Excel

ADVANCED SKILLS

ENGLISH

YEAR 3

AGES 8–9

GRAMMAR AND PUNCTUATION WORKBOOK

Get the Results You Want!

PASCAL PRESS

Laura Anderson

Reprinted 2014, 2015, 2016, 2017, 2022, 2023

ISBN 978 1 74125 399 3

Pascal Press
PO Box 250
Glebe NSW 2037
(02) 9198 1748
www.pascalpress.com.au

Publisher: Vivienne Joannou
Project editor: Mark Dixon
Edited by Christine Eslick
Reviewed by Dale Little and Kristine Brown
Cover and page design by DiZign Pty Ltd
Typeset by lj Design (Julianne Billington)
Printed by Vivar Printing/Green Giant Press

Contents

To the student

This book explains the rules of grammar and punctuation that you need for Year 3.

Each unit focuses on two or more grammar rules. Before each rule is explained, there is a text that lets you see how the rule works in everyday writing. These texts are important as they are models of the different text types and will help you in your own writing. At the end of each unit there is also a short NAPLAN-style test that lets you see how well you have understood the grammar rules.

Most of the activities can be written in this book, but you will have to use your own paper for the writing activity at the end of each unit. I suggest you buy a notebook or folder for this. The writing activities are very important. The more you do, the faster your English will improve. If you are not sure how to write something, use the example texts as a model.

It is important that you work through this book from Unit 1 to the end. This will help you build your skills and become a more confident speaker and writer of English. Make sure that you understand the work in each unit before you go on to the next one. Remember to have a dictionary handy as you work through the book, and to ask for help if you need it. There is a glossary on page 91 that explains the grammatical terms used in the units.

I hope you enjoy reading the texts and doing all the activities.

Good luck!

Laura Anderson

About this book

This book consists of fifteen units, each covering one or more aspects of grammar or punctuation. Each unit is theme-based and contains two texts designed to introduce the grammatical features and to show students how they function in context. These are followed by detailed explanations of how and why the grammar features are used, as well as exercises that allow students to put the knowledge they have acquired into practice. As an aid to revision, there is a glossary at the end of the book that summarises the grammatical terms used in the units.

The exercises in the units are organised as follows:

Let's find them!

- These exercises require students to find examples of the grammatical feature in question in the texts. They are straightforward exercises designed to test recall.

Let's go to the next step!

- This set of exercises is more difficult, requiring students to apply the knowledge they have acquired.

Let's aim high now!

- These are challenging exercises, again requiring students to apply what they have learnt.

Let's put it all together now!

- This is an editing exercise designed to test the students' understanding of the material covered in the whole unit. It also acts as a revision exercise.

Let's have fun!

- Although this exercise is designed to be fun, it is also challenging. It reinforces the material learnt.

Let's have a test!

- This series of eight NAPLAN-style questions helps students revise for the NAPLAN Tests and also tests their knowledge of the material learnt in the unit as a whole. The questions are graded so that the first two fall into Band 3, with each successive pair of questions moving into the next band.

Let's write now!

- This activity encourages students to write their own text in which they use the grammar and punctuation they have learnt in the unit. The texts are based on the theme and text types featured in the unit.

Most of the exercises in this book consist of seven questions, as we believe they give students the practice they need to fully grasp the rules of grammar and punctuation.

Unit 1 Back to school

Focus
Sentences: subjects and verbs

My first day in Year 3

I arrived at school at 9 o'clock this morning. Luiz was waiting for me at the gate. We were excited to see each other after the summer holidays and had lots to talk about. We took our bags to the Year 3 classrooms. Some of our friends were already there. When the bell rang at 9:15, we walked to the shed. We were placed in our classes and introduced to our new teachers. Luiz and I are in the same class. Our new teacher is Miss Lark. She led us to our classroom. She told us we could choose our own seats on the first day. I sat next to Luiz. Miss Lark asked us about the holidays. I told about my visit to Grandpa's farm in Victoria. I like Miss Lark. I think I'm going to enjoy being in her class.

by Angelo

Sentences

- are groups of words that make sense when they stand on their own.
- are used to tell a story or anything else we want to write about.
- always start with a capital letter and end with a full stop, question mark or exclamation mark.

For example: **I arrived at school at 9 o'clock this morning.**

Let's find them!

Find and write down the **sentence** in the text that answers these questions.

1. Who was waiting for Angelo? ______________________

____

2. What did the boys do with their bags? ______________________

____

3. Where did Angelo sit? ______________________

Let's go to the next step!

These **sentences** are missing capital letters and full stops. Rewrite the sentences correctly.

1. our teacher has already taken the roll ______________________

2. the students returned to their classrooms ______________________

3. the poster about sentences fell off the wall ______________________

4. the science projects are on display in the library ______________________

5. the Year 3 boys are practising their soccer skills ______________________

6. most of the teachers park their cars in the car park ______________________

7. the circus performers are visiting the school ______________________

Let's aim high now!

These **sentences** have been split up. Shade the beginnings and endings that belong together the same colour.

Sentence beginning	Sentence ending
1 Amanda and Lara	explained the rules of basketball to us.
2 Mrs Harvey	are speaking to my teacher about my work.
3 My parents	are on the shelves.
4 Some people from the Department of Health	are the cleverest girls in the class.
5 The sports teacher	is next to the hall.
6 The new library books	is the principal of our school.
7 The music room	told us about the importance of hygiene.

My first day at a new school

Today was my first day at my new school. Mum walked with me to the office. **The principal greeted us in the reception area.** Then Mum had to fill in some forms. The secretary asked two Year 3 girls who were walking past to look after me. Mum hugged me and I went with the girls. I felt sick from nervousness. The girls were very friendly. They told me things about the school. I saw a basketball court next to a big building. I also noticed a vegetable garden with all kinds of vegetables in it. My teacher was waiting for me in the classroom. She is very kind. So are the other kids. We played on the basketball court during recess and lunch break. I think I'm going to like my new school!

by Ellen

This is another **recount**. Ellen uses **sentences** containing **subjects** and **verbs** to tell about her first day at a new school.

Sentences usually contain a **subject** and at least one **verb**. The subject is the person or thing doing the action, and the verb is the action.

For example: The principal greeted us in the reception area. The subject is **The principal** and the verb is **greeted**.

Let's find them!

Ellen's sentences all contain **subjects** who do the action.

1. Who is the person who filled in forms? ______
2. Who is the person who spoke to two Year 3 girls? ______
3. Who are the people who were friendly? ______
4. Who is the person who was waiting in the classroom? ______

Ellen's sentences also contain **verbs**, or actions.

5. What is the action that tells that Mum put her arms around Ellen? ______
6. What is the action that means the same as *saw*? ______
7. What is the action that tells what the children did on the basketball court? ______

Let's go to the next step!

Choose a **verb** from the box to complete each sentence.

share	pack	write	practise	eat	wears	sits

1. We ______________________ running in PE.
2. I ______________________ my yoghurt at recess.
3. I ______________________ my books in my bag.
4. My teacher ______________________ pretty clothes.
5. The new girl ______________________ next to me in class.
6. We ______________________ in our maths books every day.
7. I ______________________ my crayons with my best friend.

Let's aim high now!

Circle the **subject** and underline the **verb** in each sentence.

For example: (The boy) draws a picture.

1. Max asks the teacher for a pencil.
2. She drinks water from the bubbler.
3. The girls take the note to the office.
4. Mahli reads a new book every week.
5. We play handball on the playground.
6. I put my school bag next to my desk.
7. My friends help me with my homework.

Let's put it together now!

This student has not divided her **recount** into **sentences**. Fill in the capital letters and full stops to show where the sentences are.

my speech was about snakes i took my pet python to school in a bag my teacher pulled my name out of the box and I went to the front of the class i put the bag on my teacher's desk my python started to move around he poked his head out of the bag my teacher fainted

Let's have fun!

Who or what is doing the action? The pictures will help you fill in the **subjects** of these sentences.

1 ______________________ threw the ball through the classroom window.

______________________ spilled water all over her desk.

______________________ was sitting on the classroom wall.

______________________ hopped into our classroom.

What are these people doing? The pictures will help you complete the **sentences**.

2 The teacher ______________________

______________________.

The girl ______________________

______________________.

The boy ______________________

______________________.

The students ______________________

______________________.

Let's have a test!

1 Which group of words is a sentence?

- ◯ in the classroom
- ◯ the students in Year 3
- ◯ Our teacher marks our books.
- ◯ when the school bell rings

In questions 2–3, which word can be left out of the sentence?

2 The classroom was painted yellow.

- ◯ The
- ◯ classroom
- ◯ was
- ◯ painted

3 This is the book that I'm reading in class.

- ◯ This
- ◯ the
- ◯ that
- ◯ in

4 Who is the subject in this sentence?

The Year 3s and 4s play dodge ball on a Friday afternoon.

- ◯ The Year 3s
- ◯ The Year 3s and 4s
- ◯ dodge ball
- ◯ Friday afternoon

5 Which subject completes this sentence correctly?

________________ showed us a photo of her old school.

- ◯ The new boy
- ◯ Mr Smith
- ◯ The man
- ◯ The new girl

Tip! Shade the circle next to the correct answer.

6 Which subject does **not** complete this sentence correctly?

________________ attended the Athletics Carnival.

- ◯ Many parents
- ◯ Many people
- ◯ Lots of parents
- ◯ Lots people

7 Which verb completes this sentence correctly?

The student ________________ his poem to the school at assembly.

- ◯ wrote
- ◯ thought
- ◯ talked
- ◯ read

8 Which verb does **not** complete this sentence correctly?

The Year 3 girl ________________ her rubbish in the bin.

- ◯ put
- ◯ placed
- ◯ fell
- ◯ threw

Let's write now!

Write a **recount** about your first day back at school at the beginning of a new year. Remember: start your **sentences** with capital letters and end them with full stops.

Unit 2 Friends and family

Focus
Sentences: statements, questions, exclamations and commands

From: Narelle Benson
Subject: What's wrong?
Date: 18 May
To: Jemma Jones <pmjkjones@firstnetwork.com.au>

Hi Jem

I hope you're all right. Why haven't you been at school this week? Are you sick? **I wanted to phone you, but Mum said you might be sick.** I missed you in PE today. I was Jelena's partner when we practised ball skills. **When are you coming back?**

You're lucky you weren't at school today. We had to do lots of writing. Have you finished your science project yet? I handed mine in today. Are you still going to use play-doh for the teeth?

Please phone me if you can.

Lots of love, Narelle

This is an **email**. An email is a way of communicating with others. Narelle uses **statements** to give information and **questions** to ask for information while communicating with her friend, Jem.

Statements and **questions** are types of sentences.

Statements
- are sentences that give information or opinions.
- always end with a full stop (.).

For example: **I wanted to phone you, but Mum said you might be sick.**

Questions
- are sentences that ask for information or opinions.
- always end with a question mark (?).

For example: **When are you coming back?**

Let's find them!

Tip!
Questions often start with Who, What, Which, Where, When, Why and How. They can also start with a verb.

Find three **statements** and three **questions** in the text and write them down. Remember to end the statements with a full stop and the questions with a question mark.

1. ______________________________
2. ______________________________
3. ______________________________

4 ______________________________

5 ______________________________

6 ______________________________

Let's go to the next step!

Choose a word from the box to start each **statement** or **question**.

Which	When	Grandpa	What	Who	Come	My
Why	Most	Wait	Will	Grandma	How	

1 ______________ of my cousins have brown eyes.

2 ______________ twin is the better basketball player?

3 ______________ some of your friends be at the beach?

4 ______________ is celebrating his 80th birthday next week.

5 ______________ little sister will be three years old tomorrow.

6 ______________ many people in your family have blonde hair?

7 ______________ are your friends doing on Saturday afternoon?

Tip!

Don't forget the question marks.

Let's aim high now!

Change these **statements** into **questions**.

1 Statement: There are five people in my family.
Question: How ______________________________

2 Statement: Great-aunt Mathilda is the best ice skater in Dad's family.
Question: Who ______________________________

3 Statement: Arista is the best friend I've ever had.
Question: Is ______________________________

4 Statement: I met my best friend, Jono, at soccer training.
Question: Where ______________________________

5 Statement: Nikita has lots of friends at school.
Question: Does ______________________________

6 Statement: My brother is cleaning the family car.
Question: What ______________________________

7 Statement: Mum is going to the supermarket to buy groceries.
Question: Why ______________________________

Dear Gran and Gramps

Thank you for the great bike. **I can't believe you knew which one to buy!** Do you know what my friend Harry said when he saw it? What a cool bike! He never thinks anything is cool. I can't wait to show it to my other friends!

Gramps, I left something special for you to find on your birthday. **Go to the bench near the creek.** Turn right and keep walking until you come to the big rock. Look under the little ledge at the bottom of the rock. You'll find a tin with red soldiers on it. Your present is in the tin. Wait until you're sitting in your favourite chair before you open it.

How amazing is it that we have our birthdays in the same month! Tell me what you think of your present. I hope you like it as much as I like mine.

Love, Josh

This is a **letter**. A letter is another way of communicating with others. Josh uses **exclamations** to express feelings and **commands** to give instructions while communicating with his grandpa.

Exclamations

- are sentences that express strong emotions, or feelings.
- always end with an exclamation mark (!).

For example: **I can't believe you knew which one to buy!**

Commands

- are sentences that instruct someone to do something, or give an order.
- start with a verb, or action word.
- end with a full stop.

For example: **Go to the bench near the creek.**

Let's find them!

Find three **exclamations** and three **commands** in the text. (Don't use the ones in bold.) Remember to end the exclamations with an exclamation mark and the commands with a full stop.

1. ______________________________
2. ______________________________
3. ______________________________
4. ______________________________
5. ______________________________
6. ______________________________

Let's go to the next step!

Choose a word from the box to start each **exclamation** or **command**.

How	Phone	More	We	Ride
Tell	Take	When	Help	Tidy
Write	What	Our	Cook	

1. ______________ your sister wash the dishes.
2. ______________ Grandpa's dinner up to him.
3. ______________ Dad and tell him we'll be late.
4. ______________ your room before Mum gets home.
5. ______________ a beautiful house my cousins live in!
6. ______________ had a wonderful time at Uncle Henry's farm!
7. ______________ brave my little brother was on his first day at school!

Tip!
Each word starts with a capital letter because it comes at the beginning of the sentence.

Let's aim high now!

The **exclamations** show what children might think or say when their mums or dads give them these **commands**. Shade the pairs that belong together the same colour.

Commands	Exclamations
1 Take out the garbage.	How delicious is that!
2 Read this book to your little sister.	This is such a good program!
3 Taste this chocolate cake.	I'm so excited!
4 Get ready for the party.	What a disgusting job!
5 Switch off the TV.	I'll never get it right!
6 Eat your broccoli.	What a silly story!
7 Try spelling the word again.	I hate vegetables!

Let's put it together now!

This student has used the wrong punctuation marks in his letter to a friend. Use a red pen to correct them for him.

Hi Micky

When are you coming to stay with us again. We had such fun the last time you were here? Do you remember the time we fell in the mud. That was so funny? Mum says that next time you come to stay with us we might go camping? Have you ever been camping before. Write and let me know!

Your friend, Zac

Let's have fun!

1. When Jem asked Narelle a question, Narelle's answer got mixed up. Can you sort out the words on the screen so that Narelle's statement makes sense?

   Jem's question: What can I do to show that I am a good friend?

   Narelle's answer: ____

   ____

2. These four friends have different feelings about the same thing. What is each one saying? Write the exclamations in the speech bubbles.

3. What did Mum tell her children to do? Write the commands in the spaces.

__________________ __________________ __________________

__________________ __________________ __________________

Set the table.

Wipe the counters.

Wash the dishes.

Let's have a test!

1. Which sentence is a statement?
   - ◯ Who is your favourite cousin?
   - ◯ How many nieces and nephews do you have?
   - ◯ I'm only eight years old and I already have a niece and a nephew.
   - ◯ When are your grandparents coming to visit you?

2. Which sentence is a question?
   - ◯ My mum's brother is my uncle.
   - ◯ Is my aunt's son my cousin?
   - ◯ My dad's sister is my aunt.
   - ◯ My aunt's son is my cousin.

3. Fill in the punctuation mark that should come at the end of this sentence.

   Where do your great-grandparents live ______

4. Which sentence is a command?
   - ◯ What a good friend you are!
   - ◯ My mum is an amazing cook!
   - ◯ How cool is my big sister!
   - ◯ Give the newspaper to Dad.

5. Which sentence is an exclamation?
   - ◯ My friends are awesome!
   - ◯ Buy your dad a new belt for Father's Day.
   - ◯ Meet me at Gran's house.
   - ◯ Carry the parcels for Mum.

6. Fill in the punctuation mark that should come at the end of this sentence.

   My parents were very disappointed with me that day ______

7. Which punctuation shows that Myra wants to know something?
   - ◯ "Is Gran coming to stay with us."
   - ◯ "Is Gran coming to stay with us?"
   - ◯ "Is Gran coming to stay with us!"
   - ◯ "Is Gran coming to stay with us,"

8. Which punctuation shows that Todd really likes his dad's new car?
   - ◯ "I love my dad's new car."
   - ◯ "I love my dad's new car,"
   - ◯ "I love my dad's new car?"
   - ◯ "I love my dad's new car!"

Let's write now!

Write an **email** or **letter** to a friend or family member thanking them for something they have given you or done for you. Try to use **statements**, **questions**, **commands** and **exclamations** in your letter.

Unit 3 Holiday fun!

Focus

Common and proper nouns

My visit to the zoo

In the summer holidays I went to the zoo with my mum, dad and little sister. We saw lots of interesting animals, like chimpanzees, tigers, zebras and wallabies. One of my favourite activities of the day was feeding a giraffe. They've got such long necks! I also enjoyed the seal show. There was one seal that was very clever. But best of all was watching the **zookeeper** wash the elephants in the elephant enclosure. The new baby **elephant** was so cute!

We had lunch at a restaurant with an amazing view of the **harbour**. I had **meatballs** and pasta and an ice-cream for dessert.

We had to walk a lot to see all the animals. I was so tired at the end of the day, I fell asleep in the car on the way home.

by Jake

This is a **recount** like the one in Unit 1. Remember: a recount tells about things that have already happened. Jake uses **common nouns** to name general people, animals, places and things he saw at the zoo.

Nouns are the names of people, animals, places and things.

Common nouns are the general names of people, animals, places and things.

For example: **zookeeper**, **elephant**, **harbour**, **meatballs**.

Let's find them!

Find these **common nouns** in the text.

1. the name of a family member ______
2. the name of an animal that has a long neck ______
3. the name of an animal that performs in a show ______
4. the name of the place where the elephants are kept in a zoo ______
5. the name of the place where Jake and his family had lunch ______
6. the name of something Jake had for dessert ______
7. the name of something we travel around in ______

Let's go to the next step!

Choose a **common noun** from the box to complete each sentence.

captain	suitcase	hotel	snow	ball	shark	feather
eagle	road	ticket	waiter	island	spider	instructor

1. We saw a very big ______________ at the aquarium.
2. My ______________________ is packed and I am ready to go on holiday!
3. Next time we go on holiday, we are going to stay in a ______________.
4. When we arrived at the restaurant, a ______________ showed us to our table.
5. Before I boarded the plane, I had to show someone my ______________.
6. Our cruise ship stopped at a small ______________ to pick up more passengers.
7. The biggest bird we saw on our holiday in the country was an ______________.

Let's aim high now!

Decide whether these **common nouns** are the names of people, animals, places or things and then write them under the correct headings.

park	kookaburra	pilot	dingo	museum
sailor	chef	train	mother	window
umbrella	country	wombat	city	fish
koala	snake	tourist	book	lifeguard
computer	shop	diver	forest	
beach	seat	rock	monkey	

Tip! Fill in the easy ones first!

People	Animals	Places	Things

My visit to the Gold Coast

Last April I went with my family to the Gold Coast. My best friend, **Leanne**, came with us. We had lots of fun!

We stayed at a resort called Golden Surf. It was right on the beach. The weather was amazing and we swam every day, but I liked the theme parks the best.

The first theme park we visited was **Dreamworld**. My favourite rides were the **Reef Diver**, the Thunder River Rapids Ride and the Rocky Hollow Log Ride. I also enjoyed the Australian Wildlife Experience, where we saw hundreds of native animals and birds.

On the **Sunday** we visited Sea World. We saw cute penguins at the Penguin Encounter. Leanne and I really enjoyed the adventure playground at Castaway Bay, but my little brother, Amir, could have spent the whole day watching the characters from Sesame Street. He just loves Elmo!

Dad says we might go to Disneyland in **September**. How cool would that be!

by Leila

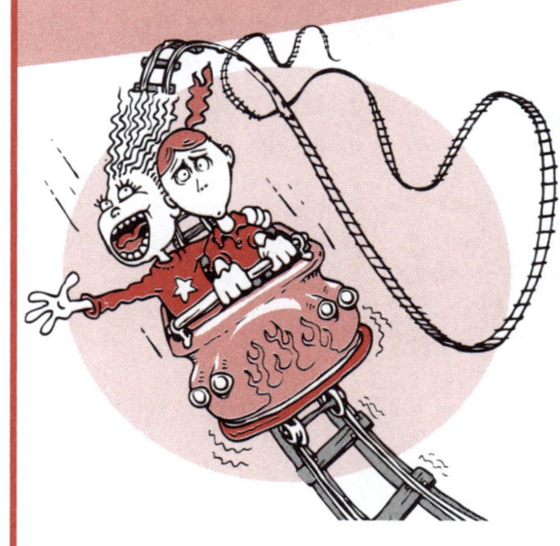

This is another **recount**. Leila uses **proper nouns** to name the particular people, places and things she saw on her holiday.

Proper nouns

- are the names of particular people, animals, places and things; for example, **Leanne**, **Dreamworld**, **Reef Diver**.
- include the names of the days of the week and months of the year; for example, **Sunday**, **September**.
- always start with a capital letter.

- If the particular name of a person, animal, place or thing has more than one word in it, all of the words start with a capital letter; for example, **Reef Diver**.

Let's find them!

Find these **proper nouns** in the text.

1. the name of the month in which Leila and her family went to the Gold Coast ____________________
2. the name of the resort at which Leila and her family stayed ____________________
3. the name of a ride where you might get wet ____________________
4. the name of a place that has a playground ____________________

5 the name of a TV program ______________________

6 the name of a character from a TV program ______________________

7 the name of the theme park Leila and her family might visit in September ______________________

Let's go to the next step!

Choose a **proper noun** from the box to complete each sentence.

Banksia Street	July	Murray River
Canberra	Tuesday	Botanic Gardens Tom

1 We leave for our holiday next week on ______________________.

2 I spent the holidays with my friend ______________________.

3 We ate a picnic lunch in the ______________________.

4 Last year we visited ______________________, which is the capital city of Australia.

5 They spent a weekend cruising down the ______________________.

6 Next year in ______________________ we are going to New Zealand on a skiing holiday.

7 Our hotel was on the corner of North Road and ______________________.

Let's aim high now!

Match these sentences from students' **recounts** with the **proper nouns** they are telling about. Shade the pairs that belong together the same colour.

Sentences from recounts	Proper nouns
1 I saw lots of interesting fish there.	Snow White
2 It is the smallest state in Australia.	Sydney
3 My best friend came on holiday with us.	October
4 We dressed up and went trick-or-treating.	Tasmania
5 Last year we visited Australia's biggest city.	Halloween
6 It was the best time of the year to see the wildflowers.	Lucy
7 In the holidays I watched a movie about my favourite fairytale character.	Waterside Aquarium

Let's put it together now!

This student has forgotten which **nouns** start with capital letters and which don't. Can you spot the seven mistakes? Use a red pen to correct them.

On the last friday of the school holidays I visited my friend Eric, who lives in Alicia street. We played computer games for a bit and then we went to a Park near his house. One of our friends from School, a boy called Jason, was also there. Jason had his little dog, juju, with him. Juju is very cute. When we started kicking a Ball around, Juju decided that he wanted to play too. He ended up in lilypad Pond!

Let's have fun!

The clues will help you work out the **common** and **proper nouns** that complete this crossword puzzle.

Tip!
You might need to look at a map of Australia to find the names of some of the places described in the clues.

Across

1. You'll see this marsupial if you visit a wildlife park.
3. If you visit Melbourne, you'll be in this state.
4. If you're on holiday in the middle of summer, you might have this healthy meal for lunch.
5. This town in the north of Queensland is sometimes called the gateway to the Great Barrier Reef.
6. If you are looking for a very hot place to visit, try the capital city of the Northern Territory.
7. Many tourists visit this famous rainforest in Queensland.

Down

1. If you travel on an aeroplane, you are one of these.
2. If you want to travel somewhere by train, you will catch it here.

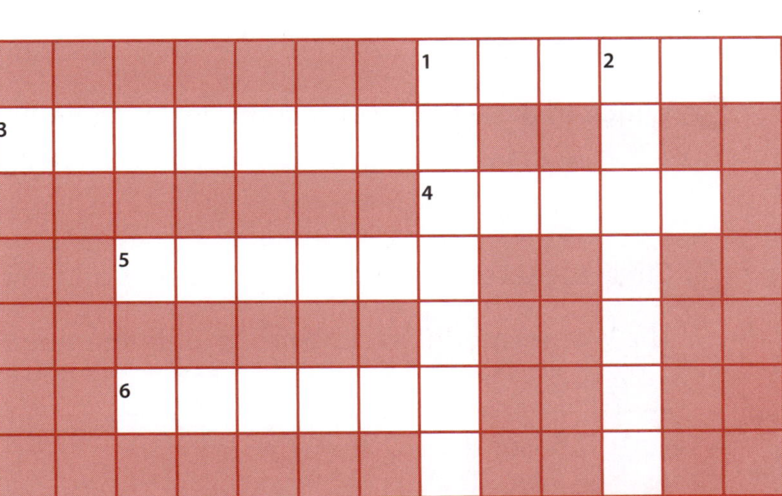

Let's have a test!

1 Which list of common nouns is a list of people?

- ◯ lion, cheetah, leopard, jaguar
- ◯ guest, visitor, traveller, sightseer
- ◯ village, town, shire, country
- ◯ canoe, yacht, kayak, lifeboat

2 Which common noun completes this sentence correctly?

We visited lots of different countries when we toured the ________________ of Europe.

- ◯ city
- ◯ ocean
- ◯ continent
- ◯ island

3 Which common noun completes this sentence correctly?

A passenger on a cruise ship sleeps in a ________________.

- ◯ tent
- ◯ hut
- ◯ room
- ◯ cabin

4 Which of these common nouns is a travel document?

- ◯ passport
- ◯ diary
- ◯ report
- ◯ file

5 Which proper noun completes this sentence correctly?

At the observatory I looked through a telescope at the planet ________________.

- ◯ China
- ◯ London
- ◯ Mars
- ◯ Lassie

6 Which of these famous tourist attractions has been written correctly?

- ◯ Nile river
- ◯ Eiffel Tower
- ◯ tower Bridge
- ◯ Empire state Building

7 Which of these tourist attractions in Australia has been written **incorrectly**?

- ◯ Great Ocean road
- ◯ Uluru
- ◯ Kangaroo Island
- ◯ Bondi Beach

8 Circle the three mistakes in this sentence and rewrite the words correctly.

The War memorial in canberra is an interesting Place to visit.

________________ ________________ ________________

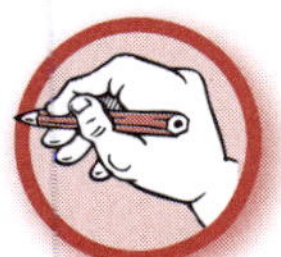

Let's write now!

Write a **recount** about a place you visited or something interesting you did on one of your holidays. Use **common** and **proper nouns** to name the people, animals, places or things that you saw.

Unit 4 In the wild

Collective nouns, compound nouns and abstract nouns

The arrival of the hunters

The **pride** of lions settled down contentedly under a shady tree. They gazed out at a herd of zebras grazing near the **waterhole**. The lions had just eaten, so the zebras were in no danger.

Sunlight filtered through the branches, casting dancing shapes on the ground. The big male swatted at a swarm of gnats swirling past him, before resting his massive head on his paw and closing his eyes. He didn't feel the light touch of the butterfly that perched on his back, or notice the flock of birds flying by. He didn't hear the grasshopper chirping in the distance. But he was immediately alert when a burst of wild chattering from a troop of monkeys shattered the stillness of the afternoon.

This is part of a **narrative**. A narrative tells a story. The author uses **collective** and **compound nouns** to name groups of animals and other animals and things in nature.

Collective nouns are the names of groups of people, animals, places and things; for example, a **pride** of lions.

Compound nouns are the names of people, animals, places and things that are formed by joining two or more words together; for example, **waterhole** is formed by joining the words **water** and **hole**.

Let's find them!

Find these **collective** and **compound nouns** in the text.

1. the name of a group of striped animals ______________________
2. the name of a group of insects near the lion ______________________
3. the name of a group of animals in the air ______________________
4. the name of a group of animals that is making a lot of noise ______________________
5. the name of something that is coming through the trees ______________________
6. the name of an insect that is colourful and light ______________________
7. the name of an insect that moves by jumping ______________________

Let's go to the next step!

Circle the **collective nouns** and underline the **compound nouns** in these sentences.
For example: A (herd) of giraffes was grazing by the <u>roadside</u>.

> **Tip!** One of the sentences contains two collective nouns.

1. In California we came across a den of rattlesnakes.
2. We collected a bundle of firewood and stacked it next to our tent.
3. A patch of wildflowers was the only bit of colour in the brown field.
4. At the beach we saw a flock of seagulls circling around a fishing boat.
5. When we looked over the side of the boat, we saw a school of jellyfish.
6. When we saw Jin Ho's album of photographs, we all wanted to go to Africa.
7. The prickle of hedgehogs crossing the road looked like moving pincushions!

Let's aim high now!

Complete these sentences with a **collective** or **compound noun** from the box. Write down what kind of noun you have selected in the space next to the sentence.

For example: A <u>swarm</u> of bees was heading our way. <u>collective noun</u>

riverbed	rainforest	sunglasses	herd
pack	library	pod	

1. I wore ________________ to protect my eyes. ________________
2. I found three books about tigers at the ________________. ________________
3. We spotted a ________________ of whales from the boat. ________________
4. We saw lots of very tall trees in the ________________. ________________
5. Some fish like to swim close to the ________________. ________________
6. The lioness growled at the ________________ of wild dogs. ________________
7. We waited for the ________________ of elephants to cross the road. ________________

Meeting the wombats

This trip had been a wonderful **opportunity** for me, but so far we hadn't seen much. Imagine my **surprise**, then, when not one, but two wombats emerged from the burrow! I'd never seen a wombat in the wild before! The two furry little creatures headed towards us. What excitement! Although I knew I shouldn't touch them, curiosity got the better of me, and I bent down to feel the smaller one's back. Although it felt a bit like touching the bristles of a brush, it still gave me a thrill. Then, to my amazement, the little wombat started nuzzling my shoe! It quickly moved away though. Maybe it didn't like the smell of my feet! The wombats were a joy to watch. My big disappointment was that I couldn't take them home with me.

This is part of another **narrative**. Remember: a narrative tells a story. The narrator uses **abstract nouns** to name the feelings she had when she saw the wombats.

Abstract nouns are the names of ideas and feelings; for example, **opportunity**, **surprise**.

Let's find them!

Find the **abstract nouns** that start with these letters in the text. (Don't choose the ones in bold.)

Tip! We cannot see or touch abstract nouns.

1. e____________________
2. c____________________
3. t____________________
4. a____________________
5. s____________________
6. j____________________
7. d____________________

Let's go to the next step!

Complete each sentence with an **abstract noun** from the box. Use each word once.

courage relief sorrow tension interest sympathy love

1. I felt ______________ when I saw the dead eagle.
2. I feel more ______________ for my pets than I do for wild animals.
3. I listened with ______________ when my teacher told us about the koalas.
4. The man showed great ______________ in fighting off the crocodile.
5. I felt ______________ when I heard they could save the injured kangaroo.
6. I felt ______________ for the tiger cubs that had been abandoned by their mother.
7. I could feel the ______________ gripping my body as the lion approached our car.

Let's aim high now!

Tip! The feelings are all abstract nouns.

Match the common saying with the feeling it shows.
Shade the pairs that belong together the same colour.

Common sayings	Feelings
1 I was **over the moon** when they let me hold the little joey.	happiness
2 I **think the world of my mum** for helping to heal sick animals.	nervousness
3 Just thinking of creepy crawlies **makes my hair stand on end**!	sadness
4 The thought of touching the hairy spider **makes my flesh crawl**.	admiration
5 I had **butterflies in my tummy** as I reached out to touch the snake.	disgust
6 We were **down in the dumps** because we didn't see any wombats.	anger
7 It **makes my blood boil** when I see how some people destroy the environment.	fear

Let's put it together now!

This student has written seven **nouns** incorrectly. Underline them and write them correctly on the lines below.

Paul and Marcie were picking a pack of flowers for Mum. Suddenly they heard a buzzing sound. They looked up and got a huge frighten when they saw a herd of bees heading towards them. Paul grabbed Marcie and pulled her towards the path way. They ran as fast as they could, but they could still hear the bees behind them. Then a swarm of birds came out of nowhere. To the children's surprising, the buzzing stopped. Paul and Marcie walked back to the play ground where Mum and Alex were waiting for them.

____________________ ____________________

____________________ ____________________

____________________ ____________________

____

Let's have fun!

1. Making up your own **collective nouns** can be fun. Which collective noun in the box is the best name for each of these groups?

tickle	squirm	squawk

a ____________ of earthworms a ____________ of cockatoos

a ____________ of feathers

2. Work out these **compound nouns** by putting together the names of the animal or thing in each pair of pictures.

+ = ____________ + = ____________

+ = ____________

3. Paul experienced different feelings when the snake handler at the reptile park draped a python around his neck. Match the name of each feeling to the expression on Paul's face and write it in the space next to the picture.

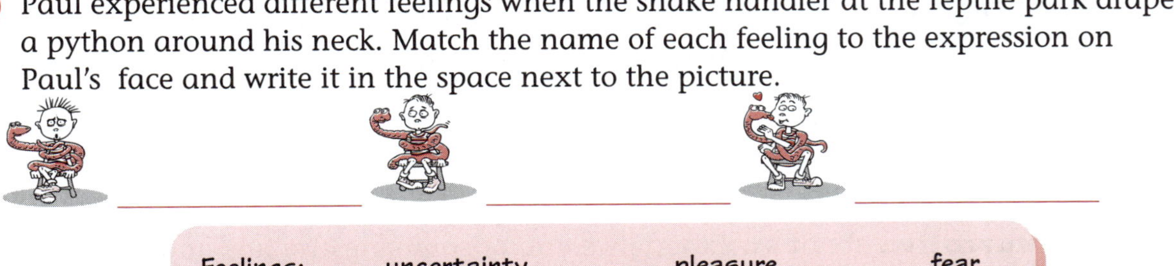

Feelings: uncertainty pleasure fear

Let's have a test!

1. Which collective noun completes this sentence correctly?
   While we were walking in the bush, we saw an ________________ of ants.
   ◯ flock ◯ pod ◯ army ◯ herd

2. Which sentence does **not** contain a collective noun?
   ◯ Suddenly a mob of kangaroos appeared from nowhere.
   ◯ The farmers were worried when they saw a cloud of locusts in the sky.
   ◯ We disturbed a colony of bats when we entered the cave.
   ◯ The white rhino is in danger of becoming extinct.

3. Which compound noun completes this sentence correctly?
   When we went to the ________________, we found lots of shells on the beach.
   ◯ seaside ◯ farmyard ◯ funfair ◯ playground

4. Which sentence does **not** contain a compound noun?
   ◯ I nearly ate a ladybug when it landed on my strawberry.
   ◯ In the movie *Finding Nemo,* Nemo is a clownfish.
   ◯ I wouldn't like to run out of water in the desert.
   ◯ We sat around the campfire and toasted marshmallows.

5. Which abstract noun completes this sentence correctly?
   To my ________________, the little animal let me stroke its furry coat.
   ◯ confusion ◯ delight ◯ disgust ◯ determination

6. Which sentence does **not** contain an abstract noun?
   ◯ The vet had a look of concern on his face.
   ◯ The conservationist looked worried.
   ◯ We watched in amusement as the tiger cubs wrestled each other.
   ◯ I looked on in admiration as the snake handler picked up the cobra.

7. Which animal's name is a compound noun?
   ◯ buffalo ◯ alligator ◯ dolphin ◯ swordfish

8. Three of the abstract nouns below have similar meanings and could be used to complete this sentence. Which noun is the odd one out?
   When Simon came face to face with the gorilla, he was filled with ________________.
   ◯ panic ◯ alarm ◯ terror ◯ calmness

Let's write now!

Write a **narrative** about an experience you or someone else has had with wild creatures. Use at least one **collective**, one **compound** and one **abstract noun**.

Unit 5 Hobbies and interests

Focus

Plural nouns

The Crazy Collections Show

The Crazy Collections Show is an unusual and interesting exhibition that's on at the Entertainment Centre until the end of May. I really liked the toy collectors' corner. There you can see collections of all kinds of **toys**, from **dolls** to miniature cars, **buses** and music boxes. I also liked the collection of superheroes, where you can see some very realistic figures of Batman and Spiderman. There is also a very valuable collection of old board games.

Some of the collections are more unusual than others. One of the exhibitors has a collection of more than two thousand brightly painted wooden walruses, while another exhibitor has over a thousand little witches in her collection of Halloween toys.

If you are a collector or are interested in unusual collections, this is the show for you.

This is a **review**. A review tells and gives opinions about books or shows. This reviewer uses **plural nouns** to refer to more than one thing that people collect.

Plural nouns are nouns that refer to more than one person, animal, place or thing; for example, **toys**.

- For most nouns, add *s*; for example, **doll → dolls**.
- For nouns that end in *s, x, z, sh* or *ch*, add *es*; for example, **bus → buses**, **fox → foxes**, **buzz → buzzes**, **bush → bushes**, **church → churches**.
- For some nouns that end in *o* and have a consonant before the *o*, add *es*; for example, **hero → heroes**.

Let's find them!

Find these **plural nouns** in the text.

1. the plural of *car* ________________
2. the plural of *box* ________________
3. the plural of *superhero* ________________
4. the plural of *figure* ________________
5. the plural of *game* ________________

6 the plural of *walrus* ______________________

7 the plural of *witch* ______________________

Let's go to the next step!

Fill in the **plurals** of these nouns; for example, **pencil → pencils**.

Singular	Plural
1 book	
2 card	
3 crayon	
4 bus	
5 leash	
6 branch	
7 bush	
8 church	
9 buzz	
10 cross	
11 dress	
12 volcano	
13 cargo	
14 tomato	

Let's aim high now!

Write the words in brackets as **plural nouns**.

1 Our neighbour builds little houses out of (match) ______________________.

2 My mum has a valuable collection of silver (hairbrush) ______________________.

3 My friend goes to a circus school and is learning how to do circus (trick) ______________________.

4 Lots of little children like to dress up and pretend they are wild (animal) ______________________.

5 My aunt once carved a whole farmyard scene out of ten raw (potato) ______________________.

6 Grandma and Grandpa spend most of their time playing (domino) ______________________.

7 I know an old woman who has a collection of old (dish) ______________________ that is worth a lot of money.

The Odd Hobbies Show

The Odd Hobbies Show, now on at the Exhibition Centre, has proved to be popular with people of all ages. It's fascinating to see the odd **hobbies** that some men, women and children have. There's a man who uses old **knives** to make chairs and tables. There are also two **children** who collect sharks' teeth and make them into little elves! Then there are the ladies who bake **bread** in the shape of fairies. My favourite, though, is the farmer who trains sheep to walk in time to music!

I found this show very entertaining and can definitely recommend it. It finishes next weekend.

This is another **review**. The reviewer uses **plural nouns** to refer to more than one person, animal or thing that can be seen at the Odd Hobbies Show.

Here are some more rules for writing **plural nouns**.

- For nouns that end in *y* and that have a consonant before the *y*, change the *y* to *i* and add *es*; for example, **hobby → hobbies**.
- For some nouns that end in *f* or *fe*, change the *f* to *v* and add *es*; for example, **knife → knives**.
- Some plural nouns are formed by changing the vowels and/or the endings; for example, **child → children**.
- Some nouns do not change their spelling when they are written in the plural; for example, **bread**.

Let's find them!

Find these **plural nouns** in the text.

1. the plural of *lady* ______
2. the plural of *fairy* ______
3. the plural of *elf* ______
4. the plural of *man* ______
5. the plural of *tooth* ______
6. the plural of *person* ______
7. the plural of *sheep* ______

Let's go to the next step!

Fill in the **plural** of each noun; for example, **story → stories**.

Singular	Plural
1 jelly	
2 supply	
3 berry	
4 curry	
5 baby	
6 city	
7 lolly	
8 fly	
9 calf	
10 leaf	
11 shelf	
12 mouse	
13 woman	
14 furniture	

Let's aim high now!

Choose the noun from the box that these people would use in their hobbies. Write its **plural noun** in the space. The first one has been done for you.

loaf	baby	sand	goldfish
pony	goose	daisy	calf

Description of hobby	Plural noun
1 Aidan likes to draw these little farmyard animals.	calves
2 Mattie often goes for rides on these little animals.	
3 Aunt Molly bakes these to sell at weekend markets.	
4 Jackie's parents raise these large birds on their farm.	
5 Lara collects these flowers and makes them into chains.	
6 Tina and Mikaela love to look after these cute little humans.	
7 Keanu keeps these little creatures in a big tank in his living room.	
8 Adilah collects it when she goes to the beach and then uses it in her artworks.	

Let's put it together now!

This student has written seven **plural nouns** incorrectly in his **review**. Circle them and write them out correctly on the lines below.

The exhibition on how to make money from hobbys is now on at the Centenary Hall. You can learn how to knit sockes to sell to friends and shops, or how to make money by selling homemade fruit loafs, cakes and cookies. You can also learn how to make rabbit hutchs to sell to pet shops. You can even get advice on making and selling jewelleries and growing organic potatos and other vegetables. This show is for all those peoples who want to make some extra money.

________________________ ________________________

________________________ ________________________

________________________ ________________________

____

Let's have fun!

Hiding in this puzzle are eight **plural nouns** that name things people can collect. The words are **glasses**, **snowglobes**, **didgeridoos**, **cards**, **paintings**, **comics**, **rugs** and **toys**. Can you find them? The words go across, down, forwards and backwards.

x	z	g	l	a	s	s	e	s	v	s	w
a	p	u	j	q	f	e	j	x	v	e	k
d	a	f	s	g	u	r	j	s	r	h	c
k	i	s	x	a	m	p	s	y	j	c	n
m	n	p	q	z	t	e	a	o	j	t	l
c	t	o	t	g	s	h	m	t	d	a	j
a	i	s	n	o	w	g	l	o	b	e	s
r	n	f	b	z	z	b	c	x	x	q	r
d	g	a	l	s	c	i	m	o	c	l	u
s	s	w	d	g	j	b	s	h	s	m	s
d	h	y	k	l	f	i	d	v	q	a	n
s	d	i	d	g	e	r	i	d	o	o	s

Let's have a test!

In questions 1–6, choose the sentence in which the plural noun has been written correctly.

1. ◯ My little sister loves to play with dolles.
   ◯ My little sister loves to play with blocks.
   ◯ My little sister loves to play with toyes.
   ◯ My little sister loves to play with her friendes.

2. ◯ I have a collection of wooden foxes.
   ◯ I have a doll that can blow kissis.
   ◯ I like to make canned peachs.
   ◯ I have a wand that lets me make wishs.

3. ◯ My dad's hobby is growing potatos.
   ◯ My dad's hobby is growing potatose.
   ◯ My dad's hobby is growing potatoese.
   ◯ My dad's hobby is growing potatoes.

4. ◯ My mum makes us fancy lollys.
   ◯ My mum makes us fancy lollies.
   ◯ My mum makes us fancy lollyies.
   ◯ My mum makes us fancy lollyes.

5. ◯ I cut the lump of clay into two halves.
   ◯ I cut the lump of clay into two halfs.
   ◯ I cut the lump of clay into two halfes.
   ◯ I cut the lump of clay into two halfves.

6. ◯ Some people collect rabbits' foots.
   ◯ Some people collect rabbits' feets.
   ◯ Some people collect rabbits' feet.
   ◯ Some people collect rabbits' footes.

In questions 7–8, choose the word that completes the sentence correctly.

7. I used my special ______________________ to cut out the card.
   ◯ scissor ◯ scissores ◯ scissors

8. My aunt's hobby is sewing decorations onto my uncle's ______________________.
   ◯ pant ◯ pantses ◯ pants

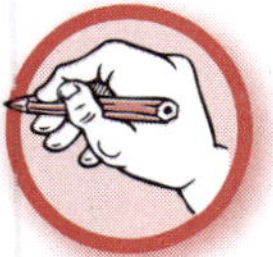

Let's write now!

Write a **review** of a show, exhibition or some other event that you have been to. Use **plural nouns** to name some of the people, animals, places or things you saw.

Unit 6 Tasty treats!

Focus
Personal and possessive pronouns

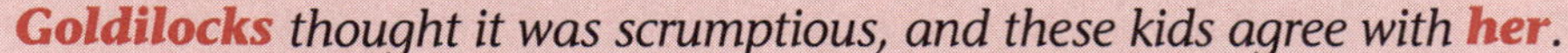

***Goldilocks** thought it was scrumptious, and these kids agree with **her**.*

This is an **advertisement**. An advertisement persuades people to buy things. This advertisement has lots of **personal pronouns** to save repeating the common and proper nouns.

What do they all love?

New Baby Bear Porridge!

Packed with nutrients and made to a recipe that **Mother Bear** created **herself**, New Baby Bear Porridge is the perfect way to start the day. Once you've tried New Baby Bear Porridge for yourself, you'll never want anything else for breakfast.

Personal pronouns

- are used in place of common and proper nouns to save repeating the nouns all the time; for example, **her** in place of **Goldilocks**.
- can refer back to a common or proper noun or another pronoun; for example, **herself** refers back to **Mother Bear**.
- can be singular or plural.

Singular	Plural
I, me, myself	we, us, ourselves
you, yourself	you, yourselves
he, him, she, her, it, himself, herself, itself	they, them, themselves

Let's find them!

Tip!

Personal pronouns that end in **self** or **selves** are also called **reflexive pronouns**.

In the text find the **personal pronoun** that is used in place of these nouns.

1. New Baby Bear Porridge ____________________
2. Sam ____________________
3. Brianna ____________________

4 Billy ______________________________

5 Tania and Andy ______________________________

6 all the kids ______________________________

Now find the **personal pronoun** that refers back to this pronoun.

7 you ______________________________

Let's go to the next step!

Choose a **personal pronoun** from the list of singular and plural pronouns on page 31 to complete each of these sentences.

1 Mum says I should eat broccoli because it's good for ______________________.

2 "Have ______________________ ever tried these lollies?" the shopkeeper asked me.

3 I promised Robert that I would give ____________________ some of Mum's apple pie.

4 Nana couldn't believe that we had baked the tarts all by ______________________.

5 We begged Grandma to give ______________ some of her delicious homemade bread.

6 Mum gave me too many cookies for recess, so I gave some of ________ to my friends.

7 Janko and Tessa will have to taste the cookies ______________________ to see if they like them.

Let's aim high now!

Replace the common or proper nouns in brackets with a **personal pronoun** from the list of singular and plural pronouns.

1 (Julie) ______________________ really wants to help Mum ice Dad's birthday cake.

2 It took (Jenny and Kate) ______________________ an hour to prepare breakfast.

3 (Daniel) ____________________ is practising his cooking skills for Junior Master Chef.

4 "(Jarred) ______________________ must finish your vegetables if you want dessert," Mum told Jarred.

5 "Whenever Mum lets us have takeaway food, I order pizza, because I love (pizza) ______________________."

6 "We don't see why (Daniel and Myrna) ______________________ can't eat gelato every day," moaned Daniel and Myrna.

7 "We'll give (Janine) ______________________ some of our lunch," said Janine's friends when Mrs Brown told them that Janine had left her lunch at home.

It's **mine**!

It's not hers.

It's not his.

It's ours!

It's not theirs.

Who is going to get the last Doggy-log?

Don't let your dog have to fight for the last Doggy-log.

Buy a jumbo pack of Doggy-logs today, and watch your dog's tail go into a spin!

Doggy-logs are rich in nutrients and their meaty flavour makes them a favourite with all breeds.

My dog loves Doggy-logs. Yours will too.

This is another **advertisement**. It contains a lot of **possessive pronouns** to save repeating the common and proper nouns.

Possessive pronouns

- are used in place of common and proper nouns to save repeating the nouns all the time; for example, **my** in place of the dog owner's name.
- show ownership, or possession; for example, It's **mine**!
- can be singular or plural.

Singular	Plural
my, mine	our, ours
your, yours	your, yours
his, her, hers, its	their, theirs

Let's find them!

Underline all the **possessive pronouns** in the text and then choose seven of them to write in the spaces below.

1. ______________________
2. ______________________
3. ______________________
4. ______________________
5. ______________________
6. ______________________
7. ______________________

Let's go to the next step!

Choose a **possessive pronoun** from the list of singular and plural pronouns on page 33 to complete each sentence.

1. I thought the chips were ____________________, so I ate them.
2. The dog stood on ____________________ hind legs and begged for a biscuit.
3. After the boys had eaten ____________________ lunch, they washed the dishes.
4. Mum told Tim that he had to eat every single pea on ____________________ plate.
5. "____________________ cheese crackers are tastier than yours," said Jing and Lan.
6. We knew the sandwiches were ____________________ because they had our names on them.
7. Mum made chocolate mousse for Sophia's birthday because she knew it was ____________________ favourite dessert.

Let's aim high now!

Replace the common or proper nouns in brackets with a **possessive pronoun** from the list of singular and plural pronouns.

1. "Don't eat that cherry pie, it's (Dad's) ____________________," said Dad.
2. The little dog eventually found (the little dog's) ____________________ bone.
3. Vanessa said that the cream cake was (Vanessa's) ____________________.
4. "Is this apple (Murray's) ____________________?" the teacher asked Murray.
5. Lots of animal trainers give (the animal trainers') ____________________ animals treats.
6. Nick and Angela bought the lollies, so the lollies are (Nick and Angela's) ____________________.
7. Aunt Jessica will show you where she keeps all (Aunt Jessica's) ____________________ tasty treats.

Let's put it together now!

The Year 3s have written seven **personal** and **possessive pronouns** incorrectly on this poster advertising their gobstopper stall. Circle the mistakes and write them correctly. There is one mistake on each line.

Get you gobstoppers here. Only $2 for a packet of eight. ______

Michael will show you how he fits six gobstoppers into him mouth ______

at once, and Emma will show you hers exploding gobstoppers. ______

Us have the tastiest and most colourful gobstoppers. Year 6 ______

think them have the biggest and best gobstoppers, but they are ______

wrong. Our are better, and a lot more fun. Try our gobstoppers ______

for youself. You won't be sorry. ______

Let's have fun!

Write the sentences next to the picture they describe. Underline the **personal pronouns** and put circles around the **possessive pronouns**.

1 ______

2 ______

3 ______

4 ______

5 ______

Mum was cross with him because he ate all the spaghetti.

My chocolate cake is sweeter than hers.

She would not finish her broccoli.

I ate the pizza slice because it was mine.

The cereal is in its usual place in the cupboard.

Let's have a test!

1. Which sentence has been written correctly?
   - ◯ I will buy they an ice-cream when we go to the shops.
   - ◯ Me will buy them an ice-cream when we go to the shops.
   - ◯ I will buy them an ice-cream when we go to the shops.
   - ◯ I will buy them an ice-cream when us go to the shops.

2. Which sentence has **not** been written correctly?
   - ◯ I like sweet food and you like savoury food.
   - ◯ We like sweet food and they like savoury food.
   - ◯ He likes sweet food and she likes savoury food.
   - ◯ Me likes sweet food and him likes savoury food.

In questions 3–4, which word completes the sentence correctly?

3. The little boy set out the food for the picnic all by ________________.
   ◯ herself ◯ himself ◯ itself ◯ myself

4. Give the buns to ________________ and we will eat them.
   ◯ us ◯ you ◯ them ◯ they

5. Which sentence has been written correctly?
   - ◯ My dad makes he's own sausages.
   - ◯ Mine dad makes his own sausages.
   - ◯ My dad makes his own sausages.
   - ◯ Mine dad makes he's own sausages.

6. Which sentence has been written **incorrectly**?
   - ◯ Your blueberry muffins have more fruit in them than their.
   - ◯ Your blueberry muffins have more fruit in them than theirs.
   - ◯ Their blueberry muffins have more fruit in them than yours.
   - ◯ Your blueberry muffins have more fruit in them than ours.

7. Which word completes this sentence correctly?

   Give them their jelly and put ________________ in the fridge.

   ◯ our ◯ theirs ◯ your ◯ ours

8. Which pair of words can be used in place of the names in bold?

   Anna's recipe for crème caramel is richer than **John's**.

   ◯ Her, him ◯ His, her ◯ My, mine ◯ Her, his

Let's write now!

Create an **advertisement** to persuade people to buy something you like to eat. Use **personal** and **possessive pronouns** in your advertisement.

Unit 7 Interesting characters

Focus

Descriptive adjectives and adjectives that compare

The Wizard of Oz

When Dorothy lands in Oz, she is met by some interesting characters called Munchkins. The Munchkins are **short** people who wear **round** hats that rise to a point, with **little** tinkling bells around the brims. One of the women has on a long, white gown. She has a wrinkled face and walks rather stiffly. Then Dorothy meets a **friendly** Scarecrow. Its head is made from a small sack stuffed with straw and it is wearing a faded suit. There is an old, pointed blue hat perched on its head. Dorothy also meets a Tin Man, who is rusted and needs to be oiled, and a Cowardly Lion, who has a terrible roar and sharp claws but is sad because he is a coward.
by Toni

This is a **description**. A description helps us to form mind pictures of people, places and things. Toni uses **adjectives** to describe characters from the novel *The Wonderful Wizard of Oz*.

Adjectives are describing words. They describe

- the appearance, shape, size, sound, taste or colour of nouns and pronouns; for example, **short** people, **round** hats, **little** bells.
- a person or character's feelings or qualities; for example, **friendly** Scarecrow.

Let's find them!

Find these **adjectives** in the text.

1. the adjective that describes the colour of the woman's gown ______________
2. the adjective that describes the appearance of the woman's face ______________
3. the adjective that describes the size of the sack that was the Scarecrow's head ______________
4. the adjective that describes the shape of the hat on the Scarecrow's head ______________
5. the adjective that describes the colour of the hat on the Scarecrow's head ______________

6 the adjective that describes the sound of the Cowardly Lion's roar ______________________

7 the adjective that describes the Cowardly Lion's feelings ______________________

Let's go to the next step!

Circle the **adjectives** in these sentences.

For example: Goldilocks ate the delicious porridge.

1 This is a story about a huge giant.

2 The wolf wanted to catch the pink pigs.

3 Why do pirates sometimes wear puffy pants?

4 Humpty Dumpty hit the ground with a loud crash!

5 The dwarfs lived in a crooked house in the woods.

6 A kind fairy helped Cinderella get ready for the ball.

7 Cinderella was unhappy when she couldn't go to the ball.

Let's aim high now!

Match the **adjectives** in the sentences with the adjectives in the other column. Shade the pairs that belong together the same colour.

Tip! The adjectives in the sentences are in bold.

Sentences	Similar adjectives
1 Captain Hook is an **evil** pirate.	courageous
2 Young Andy thought he was a **brilliant** practical joker.	risky
3 James Henry Trotter was forced to live with two **horrible** aunts.	excellent
4 Lief is the **brave** hero in Emily Rodda's book *The Forests of Silence*.	wicked
5 Beatrix Potter wrote a book about a **mischievous** little rabbit called Peter.	good-looking
6 In the fairy tale *Beauty and the Beast*, the Beast is really a **handsome** prince.	awful
7 Harry Potter faces many **dangerous** challenges in his quest to defeat Lord Voldemort.	naughty

Alice in Wonderland

While sitting on a bank with her older sister, Alice feels herself dozing off. She sees a White Rabbit rushing by and follows it down a hole into Wonderland, where she meets the weirdest characters.

One of the **odd** characters Alice meets is a talking mouse. An even **odder** character is a caterpillar who smokes a hookah. But the **oddest** of all are a Dormouse and a Mad Hatter who have a never-ending tea party.

Alice also meets a grinning Cheshire Cat, who is quite scary, and a nasty Queen, who is even scarier! Another strange thing is that in Wonderland, Alice can make herself taller or shorter just by nibbling on a mushroom! At her smallest, she is only a few inches high, and at her largest, she is nine feet high!
by Kai

This is another **description**. Kai uses **adjectives** to compare the characters in Lewis Carroll's novel *Alice in Wonderland.*

Adjectives can compare people, animals, places and things with each other; for example, **odd, odder, oddest**.

- If two people, animals, places or things are being compared, the adjective usually ends in *er*; for example, **odder**.
- If more than two people, animals, places or things are being compared, the adjective usually ends in *est*; for example, **oddest**.

Let's find them!

Find these **adjectives** in the text.

1. the adjective that compares Alice and her sister's ages ____________
2. the adjective that compares the characters in Wonderland with all other characters ____________
3. the adjective that compares the Queen with the Cheshire Cat ____________
4. two adjectives that compare Alice's height at different times

____________ ____________

5. two adjectives that compare Alice's size at different times

____________ ____________

Let's go to the next step!

Complete this table of **adjectives** that can be used to **compare** two or more characters. The first one has been done for you.

One character	Two characters	More than two characters
quiet	quieter	quietest
strong		
	larger	
		happiest
thin		
mean		
		wildest
	crueller	

Let's aim high now!

Complete these sentences by writing the correct form of the **adjective** in brackets.

For example: Father Bear's porridge was (hot) hotter than Baby Bear's.

1. Of the seven dwarfs, Doc is the (clever) ______________________________.
2. Snow White is (pretty) ______________________________ than her stepmother.
3. The (tiny) ______________________________ of all the fairies can fit into a nutshell.
4. One of Cinderella's stepsisters is (ugly) ______________________________ than the other.
5. The giant's castle was (grand) ______________________________ than the prince's palace.
6. The very hungry caterpillar is the (hungry) ______________________________ caterpillar of all.
7. Red Riding Hood said that Grandma's teeth were the (big) ______________________________ she'd ever seen.

Let's put it together now!

This student has written seven **adjectives** incorrectly in her **description** of a giant called Broc. The mistakes are in bold. Write the words correctly on the lines below.

Of all the giants in the land of the giants, Broc was the **big**. He was so **bigger** that he towered above the tallest trees. He was also very **hairiest**! He even had hair growing between his toes! But a funny thing about Broc was his feet. They were very **smaller**! They were **small** than his hands. This meant that Broc often toppled over. The crash he made was **loud** than an earthquake. Because Broc was the **heavy** giant in the land, it took six other giants to pick him up.

______________________ ______________________

______________________ ______________________

______________________ ______________________

____

Let's have fun!

Help Dorothy find her way to the Wizard of Oz by colouring the **adjectives** yellow. Remember: adjectives are words that describe someone or something.

hill dog fancy calm

tree crow witch happy

hut man sad castle

book path hat nasty lion sun

river wizard bridge excited gate food

wheat jealous scared clouds farmer

START HERE ➤ friendly house dress wind

Let's have a test!

1. Which sentence contains an adjective?

   ◯ Toto is Dorothy's dog in *The Wizard of Oz.*
   ◯ Toto is Dorothy's adorable dog in *The Wizard of Oz.*
   ◯ Toto is a character from *The Wizard of Oz.*
   ◯ Toto is Dorothy's companion in *The Wizard of Oz.*

2. Which sentence does **not** contain an adjective?

   ◯ This book is about a good witch. ◯ Some books are about bad witches.
   ◯ I have just read a book about witches and wizards.
   ◯ I liked the book about the funny witches and wizards.

3. Circle the adjective in this sentence.

   Dorothy is told to follow a yellow road that is made of bricks.

4. Which adjective answers this sentence correctly?

   What shape is the witch's house? It is ____________________.

   ◯ gentle ◯ blue ◯ powerful ◯ square

5. Which sentence has been written correctly?

   ◯ The wizard's hair was white than the witch's.
   ◯ The wizard's robe was longest than the witch's.
   ◯ The wizard's house was bigger than the witch's.
   ◯ The wizard's hat was tallest than the witch's.

6. Which sentence is closest in meaning to these two sentences?

   The girl in this story is very naughty. She's always in trouble.

   ◯ The girl in this story is always naughty.
   ◯ The naughty girl in this story is always in trouble.
   ◯ The naughty girl is always in trouble.
   ◯ The girl in this story is always in trouble.

7. Circle the adjectives in this sentence.

   The woodcutter lived in the smallest cottage in the darkest wood.

8. Which adjective completes this sentence correctly?

   The fairy was ____________________ than the witch.

   ◯ wise ◯ wiser ◯ wisest

Let's write now!

Write a **description** of a character from a book you have read, or make up an interesting character to write about. Use **adjectives** to describe and compare people, places, animals or things in your description.

Unit 8 Caring for the environment

Focus
Number adjectives; articles; noun groups

Why we must save the rainforests

Many rainforests are being chopped down. A world without rainforests will be bad for all of us.

One reason why we need rainforests is to stop us having more droughts.

A second reason is that **the** rainforests are home to lots of plants and animals. More than fifty percent of plant and animal species on Earth live in rainforests.

In the third place, many of our medicines come from plants found only in rainforests.

We have no choice. We must save our rainforests. If we destroy them, we might end up destroying the earth.

by Ella

This is an **exposition**. An exposition is an argument for or against something. In her exposition, Ella uses **number adjectives** and **articles** to introduce nouns while supporting her arguments for saving the rainforests.

Number adjectives
- show how many; for example, **Many** rainforests.
- are often used to introduce nouns; for example; **One** reason.

Articles are the words **a**, **an** and **the**. They introduce nouns; for example, **the** rainforests.

Tip!
Use **a** before a word that starts with a consonant; for example, **a rainforest**. Use **an** in front of a word that starts with a vowel; for example, **an animal**.

Let's find them!

Find these **number adjectives** and **articles** in the text.

1. the number adjective that comes before *droughts* __________
2. the number adjective that comes before *reason* __________
3. the number adjective that comes before *percent* __________
4. the number adjective that comes before *place* __________

5 the number adjective that comes before *choice* ____________________

6 an article that comes before *world* ____________________

7 an article that comes before *earth* ____________________

Let's go to the next step!

Choose the word in brackets that completes each sentence correctly.

For example: We saw (a/an) an emu in the desert.

1 Not (the/all) ____________ animals are protected.

2 (The/Many) ____________ bushfire destroyed lots of homes.

3 (A/The) ____________ eucalyptus trees surrounded us on all sides.

4 They spotted (some/a) ____________ whales in the marine park.

5 We counted (seven/one) ____________ koalas in the nature reserve.

6 I remember the (first/few) ____________ time I saw a dingo in the wild.

7 (An/Most) ____________ people think we should care for the environment.

Tip!

The articles **a** and **an** can only be used before singular nouns; for example, **a bird**, **an ocean**. The article **the** can be used before singular and plural nouns; for example, **the tree**, **the trees**.

Let's aim high now!

Complete these sentences with a **number adjective** or **article** from the box. Use each word once.

an	one	few	any
the	three	some	

Tip!

Remember to start words at the beginning of the sentence with a capital letter!

1 Very ____________ people are able to recycle everything.

2 ____________ day we might be able to recycle everything.

3 ____________ people think that plastic bags should be banned.

4 If we all make ____________ effort, we can save the environment.

5 We managed to rescue two of the ____________ penguins from the polluted water.

6 There won't be ____________ rainforests left if we keep on destroying them.

7 These are ____________ reasons that we need to look after the environment.

We need more plants!

Good morning, Mr Beckett and Year 3.

Today I will be telling the class why we need more plants around the school.

If we plant **some tall trees** along the fence at the end of the playground, there will be more shady areas for the younger children to play in. Also, if we plant a few bushes next to the shed, it will hide the grey concrete wall that runs down the side of the playground. We should also plant some pretty, colourful flowers in front of Miss Johnson's office to make the front entrance look brighter.

If we put some extra plants around the school, it will make it a better environment for the students to work and play in. It may even bring some interesting wildlife into the school grounds.

by Kyle

This is a **speech**. A speech expresses an opinion. It is a type of exposition. Kyle uses **noun groups** to tell who or what is involved in putting more plants around the school.

Noun groups
- are groups of words that are built around nouns; for example, **some tall trees**.
- tell who or what is involved in a sentence.

Let's find them!

Find these **noun groups** in the text. The first one has been done for you.

Tip! Noun groups can have articles, pronouns or adjectives before the noun.

1. the noun group built around the noun *areas* more shady areas
2. the noun group built around the noun *children* ______________
3. the noun group built around the noun *bushes* ______________
4. the noun group built around the noun *wall* ______________
5. the noun group built around the noun *flowers* ______________
6. the noun group built around the noun *environment* ______________
7. the noun group built around the noun *wildlife* ______________

Let's go to the next step!

Circle the **noun groups** in these sentences.

For example: He has a large, colourful garden.

1. They planted two little bushes.
2. She pulled out the ugly weeds.
3. This is my little vegetable patch.
4. He recycled the old newspapers.
5. We built a small concrete birdbath.
6. They counted ten green, shady trees.
7. Yesterday we visited my favourite park.

Let's aim high now!

Complete these sentences with a **noun group** from the box.

all the water	the two little joeys	the glass bottles	five old factories
a few kind people	large, leafy trees	a big green tank	

1. We collect rainwater in ______________________________.
2. They saved ______________________________ whose mother died.
3. Birds like to live in ______________________________.
4. I will recycle ______________________________.
5. We told them not to use ______________________________.
6. The smoke comes from ______________________________.
7. ______________________________ helped us clear away the rubbish.

Let's put it together now!

This student has written some of the **articles** and **number adjectives** in his speech incorrectly. The mistakes are in the **noun groups** in bold. Circle the mistakes and write the corrections on the lines below.

Water is **an very precious resource**. We should all be trying to save it. **No living things** need water. Without water we will all die. There are things we can do to save water. **A important thing** we can do is turn off the tap when we are not using it. We should also fix **a leaking taps**. If we remember to do **these one things**, we will save a lot of water. There are also **any other things** we can do to save water. For example, we can spend **the shorter time** in the shower.

Let's have fun!

The letters of some of the words in these **noun groups** have got mixed up. Unscramble them and write the words correctly.

Things we can do to care for the environment

Don't produce **so much barggae** because it ends up in landfills. ______

If we take **too many long, hot wohsres**, we waste water and energy. ______

Help to keep **the city etetsrs** clean by putting your rubbish in a bin. ______

Put your organic waste in **a potsmoc bin**. ______

Fix **a aligekn tap** straight away. ______

Only use **the hwsiagn machine** when you have a full load. ______

Whenever possible, print on **both diess of the page**. ______

Hang **all wet tcolhse** outside to dry instead of using a dryer. ______

Let's have a test!

In questions 1–5, which word completes the sentence correctly?

1 The litter made ______________ awful mess.
- ◯ the
- ◯ a
- ◯ an

2 We put ______________ piles of leaves on the compost heap.
- ◯ the
- ◯ a
- ◯ an

3 We have already planted four trees, so this is the ______________ one.
- ◯ five
- ◯ fourth
- ◯ fifth
- ◯ three

4 One day there may not be ______________ rainforests left.
- ◯ any
- ◯ few
- ◯ all
- ◯ no

5 There is only ______________ large tree in our garden.
- ◯ two
- ◯ one
- ◯ some
- ◯ many

In questions 6–7, which noun group completes the sentence correctly?

6 Instead of buying ______________, we decided to fix the old one.
- ◯ a new bicycle
- ◯ new bicycle
- ◯ an new bicycle
- ◯ brand new bicycle

7 We only use ______________ in our house.
- ◯ a energy-saving light bulbs
- ◯ energy-saving light bulbs
- ◯ an energy-saving light bulbs
- ◯ any energy-saving light bulbs

8 Which sentence has been written correctly?
- ◯ I use large the grocery green bags when I go shopping.
- ◯ I use grocery the large bags green when I go shopping.
- ◯ I use the large green grocery bags when I go shopping.
- ◯ I use the green grocery large bags when I go shopping.

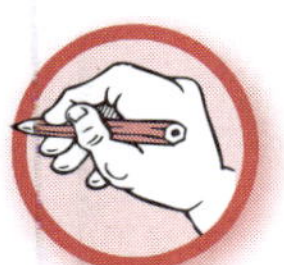

Let's write now!

Write a **speech** in which you try to persuade the students in your class that they should stop throwing away used plastic bags. Use **noun groups** that contain **articles** and **number adjectives** in your arguments.

Tip!

You may need to do some research on the damage caused by discarded plastic bags before you write your speech.

Unit 9 Doing the right thing

Focus

Doing verbs; helping verbs

These are my rules for doing the right thing in the classroom.

- Don't **interrupt**.
- **Stay** in your seat.
- Never eat in class.
- Never disturb others.
- Greet your teacher in the morning.
- Keep the area around your desk neat.
- Raise your hand before you speak.
- Always treat everyone with respect.

by Amanthi

This is a **set of rules**. A set of rules tells us how to behave. Amanthi uses lots of **doing verbs** in her rules for what students should and should not do in the classroom.

Verbs are the most important words in sentences. They tell us what the action is in a sentence. Without them, sentences don't make sense.

Doing verbs show what people, animals or things do; for example, **interrupt**, **Stay**.

Let's find them!

Find the **doing verbs** in the text that start with these letters.

1. e____________________
2. d____________________
3. g____________________
4. k____________________
5. r____________________

6 s

7 t

Let's go to the next step!

Circle the **doing verbs** in these sentences.

For example: (Speak) kindly to others.

> **Tip!**
> Be careful! Some sentences have more than one doing verb in them.

1. Always help others.
2. Put your scraps in the bin.
3. Never stand on your chair.
4. Eat with your mouth closed.
5. Wait quietly for your teacher.
6. Clean your desk if you make a mess.
7. Answer politely when someone asks you a question.

Let's aim high now!

Complete each sentence with the correct **doing verb** from the box.

thank	try	sweep	shares
play	push	tidy	

1. I always ______________________ my best.
2. My friend lets me ______________________ with her toys.
3. I always ______________________ the driveway for Dad.
4. I ______________________ my room every Saturday morning.
5. He sometimes ______________________ his lollies with me.
6. I always ______________________ people when they give me something.
7. You should never ______________________ the person standing in front of you.

How to treat others

We **can make** people feel better by doing the right thing.

- If someone is feeling lonely, we could play with them.
- If someone drops their books, we should pick them up.
- When our teacher gives us work, we must do it quietly.
- When our friends are behaving badly, we must tell them to stop.
- When someone has done well in a test, we should say "Well done".

If we remember to do these things, we will make people feel better.

by Paolo

This is another **set of rules**. Paolo uses some important **helping verbs** to help other verbs do their work in his rules for making people feel better.

Helping verbs are verbs that help other verbs do their work; for example, **can make**.

These are the helping verbs:

am	has	must	were	will
did	might	was	shall	should
may	are	had	would	does
is	have	could	do	can

If a verb consists of more than one word, it is called a **verb group**.

Let's find them!

In the text find the **helping verbs** that help these verbs.

1. feeling ______________________
2. play ______________________
3. pick up ______________________

4. do ______________________________

5. behaving ______________________________

6. done ______________________________

7. make ______________________________

Let's go to the next step!

Circle the **helping verbs** in these sentences.

For example: I (am) peeling the potatoes for Mum.

1. I will visit my sick friend.
2. We must listen to our parents.
3. She has finished all her chores.
4. I could carry those parcels for you.
5. He may show me how to play chess.
6. The children were helping the old man.
7. You should do your homework before you watch TV.

Let's aim high now!

Sometimes there is another word between a verb and its helper; for example, He **is** not **behaving** very well. Find the **verb group** in each sentence. The first one has been done for you.

1. You should sometimes take a break. ______ should take ______
2. She was probably trying to help you. ______________________________
3. They are always working on their project. ______________________________
4. Dad will never let us watch that program! ______________________________
5. Did you take out the garbage this morning? ______________________________
6. I do not like it when people are mean to each other. ______________________________
7. I have often seen him playing with his little brother. ______________________________

Let's put it together now!

This student has left out these **doing** and **helping verbs** in her rules for having friends over.

is	must	do	fight	thank	ask	share

Can you help her fill them in? Remember that words at the beginning of sentences must start with a capital letter.

Rules for having friends over

____________________ not kick balls near windows.

Do not ____________________ with your friends.

Bad behaviour ____________________ not allowed.

____________________ your toys with your friends.

____________________ before taking food from the fridge.

You ____________________ clean up if you make a mess.

____________________ your friends for coming to play with you.

Let's have fun!

Find the words! Hiding in the wordsearch puzzle are the four doing verbs **help**, **care**, **listen** and **try**, and the four helping verbs **must**, **have**, **should** and **might**. The words go forwards, backwards, up and down.

s	x	g	h	z	m	u	s	t	p
h	s	t	j	u	q	j	m	y	u
o	r	z	s	a	d	m	v	l	e
u	m	b	h	a	v	e	t	y	n
l	i	r	p	w	i	n	t	p	e
d	g	d	e	n	e	r	o	g	t
r	h	c	s	q	v	d	z	t	s
c	t	o	d	h	y	r	t	k	i
x	r	u	w	p	d	a	v	j	l
c	a	r	e	e	p	l	e	h	r

Let's have a test!

In questions 1–2, choose the word that completes the sentence correctly.

1 She always ______________________ us politely.

○ sees ○ talks ○ greets ○ cares

2 I often ______________________ him my bicycle.

○ lend ○ ride ○ borrow ○ push

In questions 3–4, choose the word that does **not** complete the sentence correctly.

3 ______________________ your toys in the box.

○ Put ○ Step ○ Place ○ Pack

4 ______________________ your aunt a thank you note.

○ Write ○ Make ○ Send ○ Walk

5 Choose the word that completes the sentence correctly.

He ______________________ not always listen in class.

○ were ○ does
○ have ○ was

6 Choose the word that does **not** complete the sentence correctly.

You ______________________ not slurp your drink.

○ should ○ will
○ has ○ may

7 Choose the sentence that contains a helping verb.

○ They play with their pets.
○ They love their pets.
○ They feed their pets.
○ They should care for their pets.

8 Choose the sentence that does **not** contain a helping verb.

○ She will help me with the task.
○ She helps me with the task.
○ She is helping me with the task.
○ She can help me with the task.

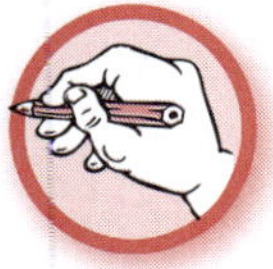

Let's write now!

Write a **set of rules** for how people should behave in a park, on a beach, or in some other public place. Use **doing and helping verbs** in your sentences.

Unit 10 Sporting heroes

Focus

Saying verbs; being and having verbs

Non-stop around the world

On 15 May 2010 Jessica Watson became the youngest person to sail non-stop around the world. People **shouted** and cheered as her little yacht sailed into Sydney Harbour. This is what some of the people had to say about her.

"She is a hero," announced one of the officials.

"She is so brave," whispered eight-year-old Frieda Fisher.

"We are very proud of her!" exclaimed her friends.

Many people told Jessica that she was special. She replied that she was just an ordinary girl.

by Charissa

This is a **report**. A report gives information. Charissa uses **saying verbs** to show the different ways people said things about Jessica Watson.

Saying verbs are doing verbs that express different ways of saying or communicating; for example, **shouted**.

Let's find them!

Find seven **saying verbs** in the text. Don't use *shouted*.

1. ______________________
2. ______________________
3. ______________________
4. ______________________
5. ______________________
6. ______________________
7. ______________________

Let's go to the next step!

Circle the **saying verbs** in these sentences.
For example, "He's going to win!" screamed his fans.

1. He moaned when he saw his low score.
2. "I'll be a champion one day," promised Jana.
3. "You need to practise more," explained the coach.
4. "We don't like doing sit-ups," grumbled the soccer players.
5. "I hope I clear the hurdles this time," murmured the athlete.
6. "I think I've swallowed the whole pool," coughed the swimmer.
7. "Be careful! They have an excellent team," warned their coach.

Let's aim high now!

Complete each sentence with a **saying verb** from the box.
Use each word once only.

sighed	called	spoke	asked	argued	answered	whined

1. "I wish I could sail around the world," ______________ Judi.
2. "Well done, Jessica," ______________ someone in the crowd.
3. "Would you like to be a sporting hero?" ______________ Sammy.
4. "I'll never be a sporting hero," ______________ the little girl.
5. "Yes, I would like to be a sporting hero," ______________ Jackie.
6. "You're too young to sail around the world," ______________ the man.
7. While at sea, Jessica Watson ______________ to her parents every day.

Going for gold!

Cathy Freeman **is** a wonderful role model. She is one of Australia's greatest athletes. At the 2000 Olympics in Sydney, there was pressure on her to win the 400 m. She **had** a wonderful race. She paced herself perfectly and won Olympic gold. There were many words of praise for Cathy that night. Cathy still has many fans. I am one of them, and so are my friends. We have a message for you, Cathy—we think you are doing a great job helping young people.

by Kenny

This is another **report**. Kenny uses **being verbs** to show that people or things exist and **having verbs** to show what people have while telling about Cathy Freeman's performance at the Sydney Olympics.

Being verbs

- show that people or things exist; for example, Cathy Freeman **is** a wonderful role model.
- include the words **am**, **is**, **are**, **was**, **were**, **be**, **being** and **been**.

Having verbs

- show what people or things have; for example, She **had** a wonderful race.
- include the words **has**, **had** and **have**.

Let's find them!

Find seven **being** and **having verbs** in the text.

1. ______
2. ______
3. ______
4. ______
5. ______
6. ______
7. ______

Tip!

The verbs **be**, **being** and **been** are used with other verbs; for example, **will be**, **are being**, **has been**.

Let's go to the next step!

Circle the **being** and **having verbs** in these sentences.
For example: The athletes (were) ready.

1. I have a photograph of Cathy Freeman.
2. There is a big sporting event every week.
3. I am one of the soccer player's biggest fans.
4. I will be at the grand final to support my team.
5. They are the best basketball players in the country.
6. They had seats for the first day of the cricket match.
7. Many people think that the Sydney Olympics was the best Games ever.

Let's aim high now!

Choose a **being** or **having verb** from the box to complete each sentence.
Use each word once.

has	is	was	been	were	are	be

1. My two favourite players ____________________ in the team.
2. He has ____________________ to the Soccer World Cup.
3. That ____________________ the best race he has ever run!
4. We ____________________ happy when she won the event.
5. He ____________________ the best player in the hockey team.
6. The athlete ____________________ a good chance of winning a medal.
7. Many people are going to ____________________ at the match next week.

Let's put it together now!

This student has left out these **verbs** in his report about Cadel Evans:

exclaimed	said	commented	be
asked	is	has	

Can you help him fill them in?

Cadel Evans ______________________ one of Australia's greatest cyclists. He ______________________ admirers all over the world. This is what some people ______________________ after he won the Tour de France in 2011.

"What a fantastic cyclist!" ______________________ Mai Chan.

"Has Australia ever had a greater cyclist?" ______________________ Josh Smith.

"I don't think there will ever ______________________ a greater cyclist," ______________________ Robyn Dickson.

Let's have fun!

The clues will help you work out the **verbs** that complete this puzzle. If you need help, use a dictionary or thesaurus.

Across

1. This verb means the same as stammered.
4. What is the missing verb in this sentence?
   I ______________________ his biggest fan.
5. This verb means the same as to tell off or to reprimand.
6. What is the missing verb in this sentence?
   He ______________________ a good game.
8. This verb means the same as cried or wept.

1	2							3
							4	
	5							
						6		
			7					
			8					

Down

2. This verbs means made fun of.
3. This verb means ordered or asked for something in a harsh way.
7. What is the missing verb in this sentence?
   She ______________________ my favourite player.

Let's have a test!

1. Which sentence contains a saying verb?
   - ◯ Many people admire Jessica Watson.
   - ◯ Many people are pleased for Jessica Watson.
   - ◯ Many young sailors ask Jessica Watson for advice.
   - ◯ Many people think that Jessica Watson is a hero.
2. Which sentence does **not** contain a saying verb?
   - ◯ The crowd gasped when he missed the goal.
   - ◯ The players chatted to each other on the field.
   - ◯ We shouted encouragement to our team.
   - ◯ Our team tried hard but lost the match.
3. Which saying verb completes this sentence correctly?

   The home crowd ____________________ loudly for their team.

   ◯ whispered ◯ announced ◯ sighed ◯ cheered
4. Which sentence contains a being verb?
   - ◯ This is the best team in the league.
   - ◯ They defeated their opponents last week.
   - ◯ We might watch the match on television.
   - ◯ We hope they will play better next week.
5. Which sentence does **not** contain a being verb?
   - ◯ We watched them playing tennis.
   - ◯ They are good tennis players.
   - ◯ They have been on the tennis court for hours.
   - ◯ This is a very good tennis match.
6. Which being verb completes this sentence correctly?

   There ____________________ thousands of spectators at the match.

   ◯ was ◯ were ◯ is ◯ be
7. Which sentence contains a having verb?
   - ◯ The athlete is standing on the podium.
   - ◯ He has basketball practice this afternoon.
   - ◯ She will run in the next race.
   - ◯ We are hoping to win the grand final.
8. Which having verb completes this sentence correctly?

   She ____________________ an important netball match yesterday.

   ◯ had ◯ have ◯ has

Let's write now!

Write a **report** about a sportsperson you admire. Use **saying verbs**, **being verbs** and **having verbs** in your report.

Unit 11 The city

Focus

Subject–verb agreement; contractions

The sights and sounds of the city

Tall buildings reach to the sky.
An old red bus rattles
down the street.
People hurry to and from
work.
A flag flutters in the breeze.
Cars hoot. Sirens whine.
A clock strikes the hour.
A train rumbles by.

We love the sights and sounds
of the city!

by Jackson

This is a **poem**.
A poem uses words in imaginative ways to express ideas or to describe people or things. Jackson uses **nouns** and **verbs** to describe the sights and sounds of the city.

The subject of a sentence can be a noun or a pronoun. The subject can be

- **singular**; for example, **An old red bus**.
- **plural**; for example, **We**.

The verb in a sentence must agree with its subject. The verb

- is **singular** if the subject is singular; for example, **An old red bus rattles.**
- is **plural** if the subject is plural; for example, **We love.**

Tip!

Remember: the subject of a sentence is the person or thing doing the action.

Let's find them!

Find these **verbs** in the text.

1. the verb that tells what the tall buildings do ______________________
2. the verb that tells what the people do ______________________
3. the verb that tells what the flag does ______________________
4. the verb that tells what the cars do ______________________

5. the verb that tells what the sirens do ______________________
6. the verb that tells what the clock does ______________________
7. the verb that tells what the train does ______________________

Let's go to the next step!

Circle the **verb** in brackets that completes each sentence correctly.
For example: The man (walk, walks) to his office.

1. The shops (is, are) open today.
2. The bus (stop, stops) to pick up passengers.
3. The city lights (shine, shines) brightly at night.
4. People (is dashing, are dashing) across the street.
5. The cars (wait, waits) for the traffic lights to change.
6. They (buy, buys) their newspapers from the newsagent.
7. Children (was looking, were looking) at the toys in the shop.

Let's aim high now!

Choose the word from the box that completes each sentence correctly.

look, looks	show, shows	is, are	catch, catches
has, have	eat, eats	take, takes	

1. I ______________________ the bus driver my ticket.
2. Some ladies ______________________ big handbags.
3. They ______________________ lunch in a restaurant.
4. The lift ______________________ us to the next floor.
5. He ______________________ the train at the station.
6. The tourists ______________________ getting on the bus.
7. People ______________________ at books in the bookshop.

We're going to the city

We're going to the city
I wonder what we'll see?
I'm sure there'll be tall towers
And potted plants with flowers.

I don't think we'll see giants.
We won't see dinosaurs!
And we'd really get a fright
If we saw monsters in the night!

But the city's full of surprises
So let's just wait and see
What special treat it has
In store for you and me.

by Samantha

This is another **poem**. Samantha uses **apostrophes** to shorten words and make them easier to say in this description of what she might see in the city.

Contractions

- make words easier to say by joining two words to make one shorter word; for example, **We're** is short for **We are**.
- have apostrophes (') in place of the missing letters; for example, in **We're** the apostrophe takes the place of the **a** in **are.**

Let's find them!

Find the **contractions** of these words in the text.

1. we will ______________________
2. I am ______________________
3. there will ______________________
4. do not ______________________

5 will not ______________________________

6 we would ______________________________

7 city is ______________________________

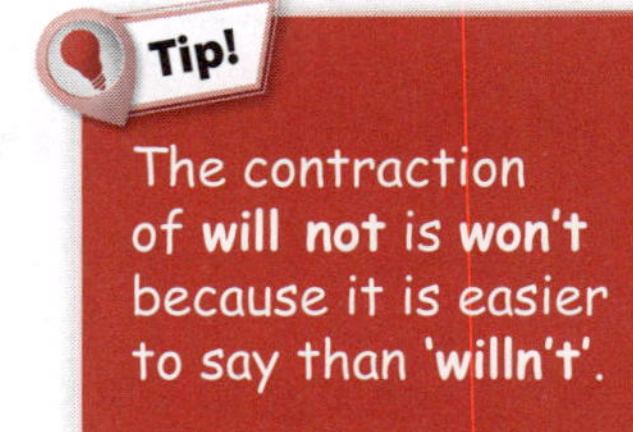

Let's go to the next step!

Match the **contractions** with the words they replace. Shade the pairs that belong together the same colour.

1 You're	She would
2 We've	He is
3 She'd	They have
4 I'd	You are
5 They've	We have
6 He's	Does not
7 Doesn't	I would

Let's aim high now!

Underline the **contractions** in these sentences and write them out in full.
For example: I've never seen so many people! I have

1 We can't go to the city today. ______________________________

2 Where's the nearest bus stop? ______________________________

3 They said they'd meet at the theatre. ______________________________

4 They're going to eat lunch in the park. ______________________________

5 She says she'll come shopping with us. ______________________________

6 He's never been in such a big city before. ______________________________

7 I didn't spend too much time in the store. ______________________________

Let's put it together now!

In this poem the student has put **apostrophes** in the wrong place and her **verbs** don't agree with their **subjects**. The words that are wrong are in bold. Can you fix them? Write them correctly on the lines.

I **do'nt** like going to the city! ______________________

This bus ride **are** uncomfortable, ______________________

I think **Im'** going to be sick. ______________________

The cars **makes** so much noise, ______________________

I think my head is going to burst.

The people **pushes** me—left and right, ______________________

I know **theyr'e** going to squash me. ______________________

Thats' why I don't like going to the city! ______________________

Let's have fun!

1. Draw lines to connect each **subject** with its **verb** from the box.

Oscar

Martin and Jerry

Veronica

Sarah and Alison

dances	catches	sing	clap

2. Sprinkle the **apostrophes** from the shaker onto the sentences. Make sure they land in the right places!

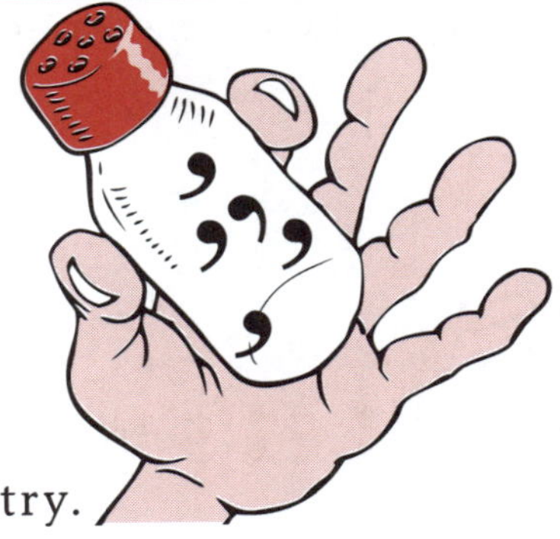

I havent been to the city for a long time.

Theres a shop in the city Id like to visit.

Its not as peaceful in the city as it is in the country.

Were going to watch the procession in the city centre.

Let's have a test!

1. Which sentence has been written correctly?
   - ◯ It are raining in the city.
   - ◯ He are walking in the rain.
   - ◯ She is holding an umbrella.
   - ◯ I think the rain have stopped.

2. Which sentence has been written **incorrectly**?
   - ◯ We visits the museum.
   - ◯ I see the dinosaur exhibit.
   - ◯ We go to the park.
   - ◯ My mother buys me an ice-cream.

3. Which two verbs could separately complete this sentence correctly?

   The man ______________ carrying a smart briefcase.
   - ◯ were
   - ◯ was
   - ◯ is
   - ◯ are

4. Which verb does **not** complete this sentence correctly?

   The children ______________ large bags.
   - ◯ have
   - ◯ carry
   - ◯ hold
   - ◯ carries

5. In which sentence has the contraction been written correctly?
   - ◯ I did'nt know where the shop was.
   - ◯ My friend said she'd tell me where the shop was.
   - ◯ I still was'nt able to find the shop.
   - ◯ I wo'nt ever be able to find the shop!

6. In which sentence has the contraction been written **incorrectly**?
   - ◯ I should've caught the red bus.
   - ◯ I knew I'd caught the wrong bus.
   - ◯ I wish the'yd told me which bus to catch.
   - ◯ I'll be more careful next time.

7. What does the contraction *I'd* stand for in this sentence?

   I'd never seen so much litter on the streets.
   - ◯ I had
   - ◯ I did
   - ◯ I would
   - ◯ I could

8. Choose the contraction that completes this sentence correctly.

   I ______________ go to the park tomorrow.
   - ◯ doesn't
   - ◯ can't
   - ◯ haven't
   - ◯ hasn't

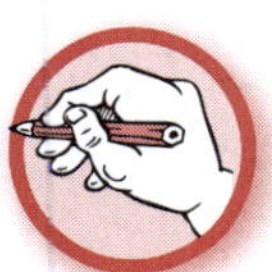

Let's write now!

Write a **poem** about the city. Remember to make your **verbs** agree with their **subjects** and try to use some **contractions**.

Unit 12 Ways of travelling

Focus
Verb tense: present, past and future

Lucinda's diary

22nd June, 1904

Last week Papa bought a horseless carriage. He **calls** it an automobile. When he **asked** me if I would like to go for a ride in it, I immediately **accepted**. It was a very bumpy ride! I **told** Papa that I did not see the point of owning an automobile when a horse can gallop faster. Papa just laughed. He said there were already quite a few automobiles on the roads, and one day everybody would be riding in them. I disagreed, and informed Papa that he had wasted his money. Dear Diary, why would people want to ride in a horseless carriage when a horse-drawn one is so much more comfortable? It seems very odd to me.

This is a **diary entry**. A diary entry is a record that people make of things that are happening or have already happened to them. Lucinda has used **present** and **past tense verbs** to tell her story.

Tense tells us when the action happens.

- **Present tense verbs** show that actions are happening at this time; for example, **calls**.
- **Past tense verbs** show that actions have already happened; for example, **asked**.

Rule!

- Many past tense verbs are formed by adding **ed**; for example, **accept → accepted**.
- Other past tense verbs change their spelling; for example, **tell → told**.

Let's find them!

Find these **past tense verbs** in the text.

1. buy ______________________
2. is ______________________
3. laugh ______________________
4. say ______________________

5. disagree ______________________________

6. inform ______________________________

7. waste ______________________________

Let's go to the next step!

Circle the **past tense verbs** in these sentences.
For example: I (parked) my car under the tree.

1. They went to China last year.
2. The little plane glided through the air.
3. The fire engine sped down the street.
4. We pushed our bicycles onto the track.
5. The bus was full of excited passengers.
6. Yesterday they caught the train to school.
7. Mum and I walked around the block several times.

Let's aim high now!

Write the verbs in brackets in the **past tense**.
Use a dictionary to help you with the spellings.

1. The first boats (are) ____________________ hollowed out logs.
2. We (go) ____________________ for a cruise around the harbour.
3. The cruise liner (sail) ____________________ to lots of little islands.
4. Last year I (fly) ____________________ to America in a big aeroplane.
5. I (stop) ____________________ to help the man change his flat tyre.
6. Last year we (drive) ____________________ from Sydney to Melbourne.
7. The man (mount) ________________ his horse and (ride) ________________ away.

Owen's journal

22 June 2011

Transport of the future

Today I found a website about the plane of the future. It **is going to be** amazing! The website says they will build the seats from a special material and the seats **will change** to fit the passengers' bodies. The passengers will see the sky all around them. Also, there will be a place where the passengers can practise their golf! Another website showed a plane that will travel from Tokyo to Paris in less than three hours. They will use fuel made from seaweed to get the plane off the ground. Then they will switch to rocket engines. The only problem is that this is going to happen in 40 years' time. I'll be an old man by then!

This is a **journal entry**. A journal is a part in a book in which we record information and ideas. Owen uses **future tense verbs** to show that actions are going to happen as he records information about the plane of the future.

Future tense verbs

- show that actions are still going to happen; for example, **is going to be**.
- can also contain the helping verb **will**; for example, **will change**.

Let's find them!

Find the **future tense** of these verbs in the text.

1. build ______________________
2. see ______________________
3. is ______________________
4. travels ______________________
5. use ______________________
6. switch ______________________
7. happen ______________________

Let's go to the next step!

Complete each sentence with a **future tense** verb group from the box.

are going to ride	will transport	will land	are going to hire
will fly	are going to sail	will drive	

1. The cars of the future ________________ themselves!
2. The aeroplane ________________ on the new runway.
3. We ________________ a car in Brisbane.
4. The cars of the future ________________ in the air and travel on the ground.
5. Next weekend we ________________ on the harbour.
6. Tomorrow we ________________ on a very fast train.
7. In the future moving sidewalks ________________ us from place to place.

Let's aim high now!

Write these sentences in the **future tense**. Use either **going to** or **will**. Start each sentence with the word or words you have been given.

For example: The horse pulls the cart.

This afternoon the horse **will pull** the cart. OR

This afternoon the horse **is going to pull** the cart.

1. My dad travels overseas. Next year ________________

____

2. We try out our new skateboards. Tomorrow morning ________________

____

3. My father rides his bicycle to work. Next month ________________

____

4. My racing bike is red, white and blue. My next racing bike ________________

____

5. My brother drives Nanna to the shops. Tomorrow ________________

____

6. My grandparents stay in their caravan. Next month ________________

____

7. The aeroplane takes off with a loud roar. Tonight ________________

____

Let's put it together now!

This student has written the **verbs** in bold in the wrong tense. Write them correctly on the lines.

22 June, 2011

Dear Diary

This morning Dad **buy** me a new scooter. It is the latest Speedy Rocket ________________

with special wheels. He **get** it at the bicycle shop in the shopping centre. ________________

He **bring** it home in a big box with a red ribbon around it. I was very ________________

excited when I **see** the big box because I knew what was inside it. Dad ________________

says he **put** it together for me tomorrow. I am so excited. The first thing ________________

I **do** is practise riding it on the driveway and around the house. Then on ________________

Saturday Dad **take** me to the park. ________________

Let's have fun!

The **verbs** and **verb groups** that show ways of travelling have fallen off the word shelf. Put them back where they belong.

Past tense verbs	Future tense verbs

are going to drive   rowed   is going to walk

cycled   will sail   will paddle   carried   flew

Let's have a test!

1. Which sentence has been written correctly?
   - ◯ Yesterday I travelled to school by bus.
   - ◯ Yesterday I travel to school by bus.
   - ◯ Yesterday I will travel to school by bus.
   - ◯ Yesterday I am going to travel to school by bus.

2. Which sentence has been written **incorrectly**?
   - ◯ I walked to the shops this morning.
   - ◯ I walked to the shops yesterday afternoon.
   - ◯ I walked to the shops tomorrow.
   - ◯ I walked to the shops last week.

3. Which verb or verb group completes this sentence correctly?

   I ______________________ off my bike the day before yesterday.

   ◯ fall ◯ will fall ◯ am going to fall ◯ fell

4. Which verb does **not** complete this sentence correctly?

   The boat ______________________ on the lake.

   ◯ sailed ◯ drift ◯ bobbed ◯ floated

5. Which sentence has been written correctly?
   - ◯ The aeroplane will land early tomorrow morning.
   - ◯ The aeroplane land early tomorrow morning.
   - ◯ The aeroplane landed early tomorrow morning.

6. Which sentence has been written **incorrectly**?
   - ◯ Next month the train will speed along the tracks.
   - ◯ Next month the train is going to speed along the tracks.
   - ◯ Next month the train sped along the tracks.

7. Which verb or verb group completes this sentence correctly?

   Next year we ______________________ to America.

   ◯ are going ◯ went ◯ gone ◯ goes

8. Which verb does **not** complete this sentence correctly?

   In the future cars ______________________ different.

   ◯ will look ◯ looked ◯ are going to look

Let's write now!

Write a **diary entry** about a journey you have made or a journey you are going to make. Use **past** and **future tense verbs** in your diary or journal entry.

Unit 13 The Dreamtime

Focus

Adverbs; phrases; prepositions

How Kangaroo got a pouch

Joey loved to explore and he **often** got lost. One day, while Mother Kangaroo was looking for him, she bumped into Wombat. Wombat yelled at her **angrily**, but Mother Kangaroo treated him kindly. She helped him find food and water. Later, Mother Kangaroo noticed some men **nearby**. They were carrying spears. She immediately picked up Joey and told Wombat to hold firmly onto her tail. Then she quickly hopped behind a big rock. They waited there until the men went away. Afterwards, Wombat rewarded Mother Kangaroo by giving her a pouch to carry her children in.

This is an Aboriginal story about the Dreamtime. It is a **folktale** (a type of narrative). The author uses **adverbs** to describe when, where and how the characters did things.

Adverbs add meaning to verbs by telling when, where or how something is done.

For example: **often** tells when Joey got lost; **nearby** tells where the men were; **angrily** tells how Wombat yelled.

Tip!

Many adverbs that tell how an action is done end in ly.

Let's find them!

Find the **adverbs** in the text that tell how, when or where.

1. how Mother Kangaroo treated Wombat ______________________
2. when Mother Kangaroo noticed the men ______________________
3. when Mother Kangaroo picked up Joey ______________________
4. how Wombat held onto Mother Kangaroo's tail ______________________

5 how Mother Kangaroo hopped ______________________

6 where the men went ______________________

7 when Wombat rewarded Mother Kangaroo ______________________

Let's go to the next step!

The **adverb** in each sentence is in bold. Fill in whether it tells when, where or how the action is done.

For example: They waited **quietly** for the men to leave. how

1 The Aboriginal elder told us to sit **here**. ______________________

2 He **proudly** showed us the Aboriginal rock art. ______________________

3 We listened **respectfully** to the old man's story. ______________________

4 The rainbow snake moved **slowly** across the land. ______________________

5 She told us the story about the didgeridoo **yesterday**. ______________________

6 I **always** like to listen to stories about the Dreamtime. ______________________

7 There are drawings about the Dreamtime **somewhere** in the cave. ______________________

Let's aim high now!

Find an **adverb** in the box to complete each sentence. The word in brackets at the end of the sentence tells you what kind of adverb to look for. Use each adverb once.

never	softly	still	everywhere
again	inside	nervously	

1 The hunters whispered ______________________ to each other. (how)

2 The kangaroos watched the hunters ______________________. (how)

3 We liked the story, so we listened to it ______________________. (when)

4 The cave was empty, so the hunters went ______________________. (where)

5 Mother Kangaroo searched ______________________ for her Joey. (where)

6 I have ______________________ heard such an interesting Dreamtime story! (when)

7 Parents ______________________ tell their children stories about the Dreamtime. (when)

Bilba the bilby

Bilba the bilby was once a man. He lived **in a sandy place** with Mayra the wind. Bilba couldn't see Mayra, so he asked him to make himself visible. Mayra refused. Bilba was angry and wouldn't go hunting in the forest with Mayra. Mayra decided to teach Bilba a lesson. He took a deep breath and raced towards Bilba with a loud roar. He whipped up a terrible windstorm around his friend. Bilba quickly buried himself under the ground. He only came out after sunset. He decided it was safer inside the sand, and that is where he lives to this day.

This is another Aboriginal story about the Dreamtime. The author uses **phrases** to add important information about Bilba the bilby.

Phrases

- are groups of words that add important information to sentences.
- do not contain a verb.
- often do the work of adverbs; for example, **in a sandy place** tells where Bilba lived.

Prepositions

- are important little words that tell us about the position of people or things.
- often come at the beginning of a phrase; for example, **in** a sandy place.

Some prepositions are:

about	before	down	of	under
above	behind	during	on	until
across	below	for	over	up
after	beneath	from	since	with
around	beside	in	through	
at	by	into	to	

Let's find them!

Find these **phrases** in the text.

1. the phrase that tells us **where** Mayra went hunting ______________________
2. the phrase that tells us **how** Mayra raced towards Bilba ______________________

3. the phrase that tells us **where** Mayra whipped up the windstorm

____

4. the phrase that tells us **where** Bilba buried himself ______________________
5. the phrase that tells us **when** Bilba came out of the ground ______________________
6. the phrase that tells us **where** Bilba felt safer ______________________
7. the phrase that tells us **how long** Bilba has lived under the ground

____

Let's go to the next step!

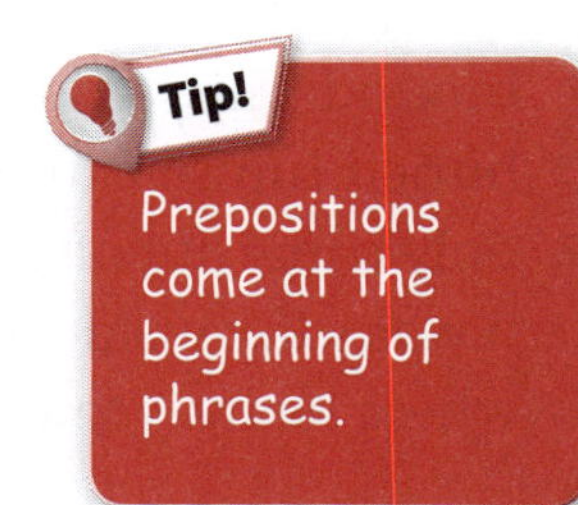

Circle the **prepositions** in these sentences.
For example: Bilba lives (below) the ground.

1. Mayra raced across the desert.
2. Bilba lived behind a rock.
3. Now Bilba lives beside the billabong.
4. Mayra went hunting before sunset.
5. I saw a bilby when we went to the zoo.
6. Sometimes the wind blows with great force.
7. Many people have seen bilbies run into their burrows.

Let's aim high now!

Complete the **phrase** in each sentence with a **preposition** from the box on page 75.
For example: The bilby ran **through the gate**.

1. Bilba was cross ______________________ **Mayra**.
2. This story is ______________________ **a little bilby**.
3. The bilby hurried ______________________ **the desert**.
4. The wind made ripples ______________________ **the lake**.
5. I haven't seen a bilby ______________________ **last year**.
6. I read the Dreamtime story ______________________ **a book**.
7. A snake slithered ______________________ **the bilby's burrow**.

Let's put it together now!

This student has left out these **adverbs** and **prepositions** in his Dreamtime story. Can you fill them in for him?

towards later on sadly of with hungrily

Two men went fishing ______________ a lake. At the end of the day, their boat was full ______________ fish. When they got to shore, they saw a stranger walking ______________ them. The stranger looked ______________ at the fish, but the men refused to share them ______________ him. The man looked at them ______________ and said they were greedy. When they cleaned the fish ______________ that day, they saw that they were full of bones.

Let's have fun!

1 Fish out an **adverb** from the billabong to show how each of these characters from the Dreamtime is performing the action.

furiously greedily snugly quickly

Joey fits ______________ in Mother Kangaroo's pouch.

To get away from the hunters, Emu ran ______________ across the open plains.

Mayra yelled ______________ as he blew up a windstorm around Bilba.

The men eyed the fish ______________.

2 Pick a **preposition** from the tree to complete each of the **phrases** in the sentences below.

towards on beside under at into across

The hunter is throwing his spear ______________ the kangaroo.

The platypus is swimming ______________ the water.

The hunter is sitting ______________ the creek.

The wombat is waddling ______________ the creek.

The kookaburra is sitting ______________ the branch.

The hunter is dropping his fishing line ______________ the water.

The hunter is walking ______________ the creek.

Let's have a test!

1. Which sentence tells when the hunter is sharpening his spear?
   - ◯ The hunter is sharpening his spear outside.
   - ◯ The hunter is sharpening his spear now.
   - ◯ The hunter is sharpening his spear carefully.
   - ◯ The hunter is sharpening his spear quietly.

2. Which sentence tells where the bilby will sleep?
   - ◯ The bilby will sleep peacefully.
   - ◯ The bilby will sleep tonight.
   - ◯ The bilby will sleep underground.
   - ◯ The bilby will sleep later.

3. Which sentence tells how the storyteller is speaking?
   - ◯ The storyteller is speaking clearly.
   - ◯ The storyteller is speaking inside.
   - ◯ The storyteller is speaking there.
   - ◯ The storyteller is speaking tomorrow.

In questions 4–6 choose the word that completes the sentence correctly.

4. The kangaroo jumps over the wall ________________.

   ◯ easy ◯ easily ◯ easier ◯ easiest

5. The men put the fish ________________ the basket.

   ◯ since ◯ in ◯ through ◯ for

6. They gave the fish ________________ the man.

   ◯ towards ◯ over ◯ to ◯ beneath

In questions 7–8 choose the word that does **not** complete each sentence correctly.

7. The wombat hurried ________________ his burrow.

   ◯ down ◯ into ◯ along ◯ until

8. The man walked ________________ the rock.

   ◯ beside ◯ across ◯ between ◯ over

Let's write now!

Research **Dreamtime stories** by finding books about them in the library or looking on the Internet. Choose one of the stories and write it in your own words. Use **adverbs** and **prepositions** in your story.

Unit 14 Paper magic

Focus
Conjunctions; apostrophes that show ownership

How to make a jellyfish

You will need a cardboard egg box, scissors, glue **or** sticky tape, paints and a paintbrush, thread and a black marker.

First, cut out a cup from the egg box.

Trim the bottom before moving on to the next step.

Paint the cup a bright colour, unless you prefer the existing colour.

After that, cut six pieces of thread, each 5 cm long.

Attach the threads along the inside of the cup, but wait for the paint to dry first.

Finally, draw a face on your jellyfish. Attach a piece of thread to the top if you want to hang it up.

I usually give my jellyfish weird faces because it makes them more interesting.

by Savina

This is a **procedure**. A procedure tells how to make or do something. Savina uses **conjunctions** to join single words and groups of words while telling how to make a jellyfish.

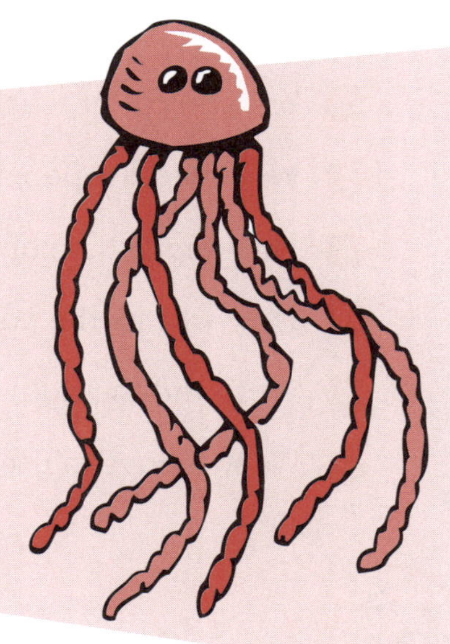

Conjunctions are little words like **and**, **or** and **but** that join single words and groups of words in sentences; for example, glue **or** sticky tape.

Here are some more conjunctions:

although	because	if	when
unless	until	so	while

Let's find them!

Find seven different **conjunctions** in the text and write them on the lines.

1 ______________________

2 ______________________

3 ______________________________

4 ______________________________

5 ______________________________

6 ______________________________

7 ______________________________

Let's go to the next step!

Underline the **conjunctions** in these sentences.
For example: I drew the patterns onto paper and cut them out.

1. You can draw pictures if you want to.
2. You can cut or tear the paper into small pieces.
3. We sorted the paper, although we didn't have to.
4. They made the paper cranes while we looked on.
5. They will set the paper out, but they won't draw on it.
6. We found the right book, so we were able to read the story.
7. We will have to use the recycled paper because it is cheaper.

Let's aim high now!

Use a **conjunction** from the box to complete each sentence.
Use each conjunction once.

so	because	or	and	when	unless	but

1. I made a paper mask ______________ a paper crown.
2. I made a paper mask ______________ you asked me to.
3. I won't make the paper mask ______________ you ask me to.
4. I've made the paper mask, ______________ you should be happy.
5. I bought the paper for the mask ______________ I went to town.
6. I made a paper mask, ______________ it is too small for my face.
7. You can have the paper mask ______________ you can have the paper crown.

How books get to readers

From the **mind's** thoughts to the writer's hand

From the merchant's ink to the craftsman's pen

From the tree's pulp to the book's pages

From the **printers'** blocks to the bookbinders' shops

From the warehouses' boxes to the libraries' shelves

That's how books get to readers.

by Luke

This is another **poem**. Luke uses **apostrophes** to show ownership while describing how books get to readers.

Apostrophes are used to show ownership; for example, **the mind's thoughts**. The apostrophe shows that the thoughts belong to the mind.

- If there is <u>one</u> owner, the apostrophe comes <u>before</u> the **s**; for example, **the mind's thoughts**.
- If there is <u>more than one</u> owner, the apostrophe comes <u>after</u> the **s**; for example, **the printers' blocks**.

Let's find them!

Find this information in the text.

1. Who or what owns the hand? ______________________
2. Who or what owns the ink? ______________________
3. Who or what owns the pen? ______________________
4. Who or what owns the pulp? ______________________
5. Who or what owns the shops? ______________________

6. Who or what owns the boxes? ______________________________

7. Who or what owns the shelves? ______________________________

Let's go to the next step!

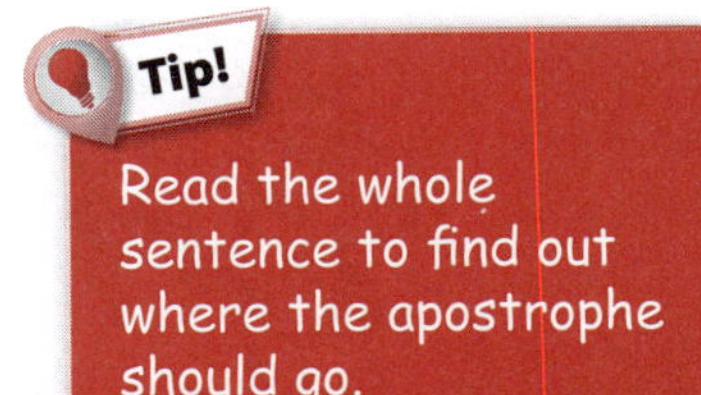

Show who the owners are in these sentences by adding the **apostrophes**.

For example: This is the **man's** bookcase.

1. Josephs paper model won first prize.
2. The students books are in their bags.
3. Melissas paper lantern is under the desk.
4. The girls lampshade is made of cardboard.
5. These boys paper aeroplanes are in the bin.
6. I flipped through the books pages to see the pictures.
7. Those artists drawings are done on a special kind of paper.

Let's aim high now!

Rewrite these sentences, using **apostrophes** to show ownership.

For example: The paper fan belongs to the lady. It is **the lady's paper fan**.

1. The paper hat belongs to Daniel. It is ______________________________
2. The labels belong to the boxes. They are ______________________________
3. The covers belong to the books. They are ______________________________
4. The machine belongs to the printer. It is ______________________________
5. The letters belong to my grandmother. They are ______________________________
6. The paperweight belongs to my sister. It is ______________________________
7. The bookmarks belong to the teachers. They are ______________________________

Let's put it together now!

This student has left out three **conjunctions** and four **apostrophes** in her poem. Can you fill them in for her? She has left out the conjunctions **and**, **but** and **if**.

The old book

My books pages are old ______________ tattered,

______________ I still love it.

The titles letters are faded and dull, but I still know what they say.

______________ I turn to my favourite picture

I can still hear my grandmothers voice telling me about the dragons treasure

in the big, wooden chest.

Let's have fun!

1. The **conjunctions** that complete these sentences are hiding in the words at the end of each sentence. Can you find them?

   For example: You can have this wrapping paper **or** that wrapping paper. (ST**OR**AGE)

   I will make you a paper aeroplane ______________ you promise not to play with it in class. (SNIFF)

   I was going to make a paper hat, ______________ I changed my mind. (REBUTTAL)

   Leigh provided the paper plates ______________ I provided the food. (HANDLE)

2. The pictures will help you complete these sentences. Don't forget the **apostrophes**!

   The ______________ bed is made of cardboard.

   The ______________ packet is going in the bin.

   The girl drew the ______________ outline on the paper.

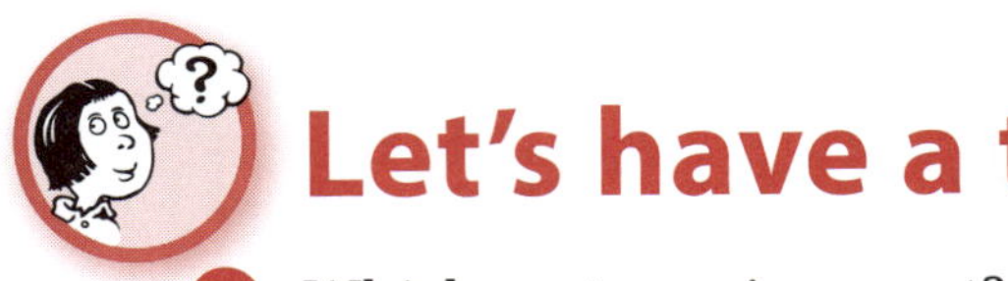

Let's have a test!

1. Which sentence is correct?
   - ◯ I have paper, or I don't have a pencil.
   - ◯ I have paper, but I don't have a pencil.
   - ◯ I have paper, when I don't have a pencil.
   - ◯ I have paper, until I don't have a pencil.

2. Which sentence is **not** correct?
   - ◯ We like this paper because it's red.
   - ◯ We like this paper and it's red.
   - ◯ We like this paper after it's red.
   - ◯ We like this paper even though it's red.

3. Which word completes this sentence correctly?

   I'll give you some paper ______________________ you behave.

   ◯ unless ◯ if ◯ first ◯ finally

4. Which word completes this sentence correctly?

   I draw the picture ______________________ I colour it in.

   ◯ until ◯ but ◯ before ◯ after

5. Which sentence is correct?
   - ◯ The girls' cards are in the envelopes.
   - ◯ The girls card's are in the envelopes.
   - ◯ The girls cards' are in the envelopes.
   - ◯ The girls cards are in the envelopes'.

6. Which sentence is **not** correct?
   - ◯ The student's books are on the shelf.
   - ◯ The students' books are on the shelf.
   - ◯ The students' books are on the shelves.
   - ◯ The students books' are on the shelves.

In questions 7–8 show where there should be an apostrophe by shading in the circle.

7. The lady◯s books◯ are in those cupboard◯s.

8. The diaries◯ page◯s are different colours◯.

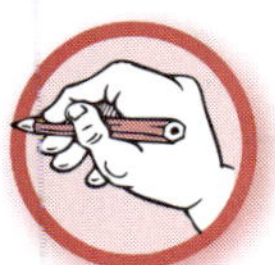

Let's write now!

Write a **procedure** that tells how to make something from paper or card. Use **conjunctions** to join single words and groups of words.

OR

Write a **poem** about your family's favourite things. Remember to use **apostrophes** correctly if you have to show ownership.

Unit 15 Pets

Focus
Speech marks; commas

A dog, or a cat?

"Should we get a dog or a cat?" asked Lena.

"A cat," replied Mum. "Dogs are a lot of work."

"I would rather have a dog," said Lena. "They're more fun to play with."

"Cats can be fun too," said Mum, "and they're cuter than dogs."

"Oh, no!" exclaimed Lena. "Little dogs are much cuter than cats!"

by Ginny

This is a type of **discussion**. A discussion looks at both sides of an argument. Ginny uses **speech marks** to show the exact words Lena and her mum use while discussing whether to get a dog or a cat.

Speech marks
- are used to show the exact words someone says.
- are placed around spoken words, including the punctuation mark; for example, **"A cat,"** replied Mum.

Tip!

A conversation between two or more people is known as **dialogue**.

Let's find them!

Write down five things that people say in the text.

For example: "I would rather have a dog,"

1. ______________________
2. ______________________
3. ______________________
4. ______________________
5. ______________________

Let's go to the next step!

Underline the spoken words in these sentences.

1. "Look at the cute little puppy!" exclaimed Jodie.

2. "Take your dog for regular walks," advised the vet.

3. Tina said, "I would rather have a canary than a mouse."

4. "How many fish have you bought for the fish tank?" asked Kamal.

5. Monica shouted, "Be careful you don't step on my pet chameleon!"

6. "I have two hermit crabs that I keep in a tank," Nick told his teacher.

7. "When are you taking your poodle to the dog parlour?" Natasha asked.

Let's aim high now!

Place **speech marks** around the spoken words in these sentences. Don't forget that the punctuation mark must also be inside the speech marks.

1. That's the puppy I want! exclaimed Kim.

2. What is your parrot's name? asked Ricky.

3. You are my best friend, said Tilda to her puppy.

4. My cat's favourite food is roast chicken, said Cara.

5. My cat coughed up a fur ball this morning, laughed Lena.

6. Did you know that Josh has stick insects for pets? asked Hugo.

7. Martin announced, I am going to the pet shop to buy my dog a new collar.

Our pets

Jono's dog likes to chew on **bones, shoes and rubber balls**.

Vinny has **a dog, a cat, a mouse and a parrot**.

Li's stick insects are called Spiky, Skinny and Scary.

Wanda's cat likes cheese, tuna and chicken.

Julie's kitten sleeps on a cushion, blanket or mat.

Lana sometimes puts a jacket, bow tie and hat on her puppy.

Neil's snake likes to curl around his fingers, wrists and arms.

Mia's mum says she can have a gerbil, a budgie or a rat.

Ollie is going to call his new puppy Elmo, Ernie or Oscar.

by 3G

In these sentences, 3G's teacher uses **commas** to separate items in lists.

Commas are used to separate items in a list; for example, **bones, shoes and rubber balls**.

Tip!

The conjunctions **and** and **or** are usually used instead of a comma to separate the last two items in the list.

Let's find them!

Write down seven lists from the text.

For example: a dog, a cat, a mouse and a parrot.

1 ______

2 ______

3 ______

4 ______

5 ______

6 ______

7 ______

Let's go to the next step!

Underline the lists in these sentences.

For example: Arthur's bird hops into his cupboard, drawers and boxes.

1. I gave the kittens to Micky, Kyle and Cassie.
2. My favourite birds are budgies, parrots and cockatoos.
3. He has bought his dog a bed, a collar and some snacks.
4. I may get a puppy, a kitten or a guinea pig for my birthday.
5. My cousin lives on a farm and has a horse, a pony and a pig.
6. There is a mattress, a blanket and a pillow in my dog's kennel.
7. When we go on holiday, my cat stays with my aunt, my gran or my friend.

Let's aim high now!

Add the **commas** that are missing from the lists in these sentences.

1. My dogs' names are Reggie Max and Molly.
2. I throw a ball stick or soft toy for my dog to fetch.
3. My favourite dogs are poodles spaniels and labradors.
4. I buy my cat's food from a pet shop supermarket or vet.
5. At the pet shop I saw goldfish mice hamsters and birds.
6. He might buy his kitten a toy a cushion or a scratching post.
7. We've taken our pets with us to Melbourne Brisbane Sydney and Perth.

Let's put it together now!

This student has left out some of the **speech marks** and **commas** in this conversation between Amanda and her mother. Can you write them in?

Why can't I have a dog, Mum? asked Amanda.

It costs a lot of money to look after a dog, replied Mum.

"We already have a bed bowl and kennel for a dog," said Amanda.

"That's from when Gran Gramps and Aunt Jo were staying here with their dog," said Mum. There are also lots of other things to buy for dogs.

Like what? asked Amanda.

"Like food medicines and toys," said Mum.

Let's have fun!

1. Write the actual words that Miles and Christine used in the speech bubbles.

   "May I hold your puppy?" asked Christine.

   "Yes, but be careful," said Miles.

2. Write the items in each picture as a list.

   For example:    a dog, a cat and a mouse

Let's have a test!

1. Which sentence has been written correctly?
   - ◯ "My cat likes to curl up on my bed, said Julian.
   - ◯ "Is your dog allowed in the house" asked Remy.
   - ◯ Tracey said, "What a cute puppy!"
   - ◯ "I'm training my dog to roll over, said Min."

2. Which sentence has been written **incorrectly**?
   - ◯ "Rats make very good pets," said the lady at the pet shop.
   - ◯ Lien said, "Guinea pigs can bite, but seldom do."
   - ◯ The vet said, Chocolate is bad for dogs."
   - ◯ "Is your gerbil tame?" asked Liam.

3. Where should the speech marks be in this sentence?

   I am going to take my dog for a walk, said Jerry.

4. Which punctuation mark belongs in the box?

   Dimitri said ☐ "I have two pets—a dog and a cat."

   ◯ ,   ◯ ?   ◯ !   ◯ .

5. Which sentence has been written correctly?
   - ◯ They have rabbits, gerbils mice and chickens.
   - ◯ They have rabbits gerbils, mice and chickens.
   - ◯ They have rabbits, gerbils, mice, and chickens.
   - ◯ They have rabbits, gerbils, mice and chickens.

6. Where should the commas be in this sentence?

   We took our dog cat canary and pet mouse with us on holiday.

7. Which sentence has been punctuated correctly?
   - ◯ "Give your dog water, food, and lots of love" said the man.
   - ◯ "Give your dog water, food and lots of love," said the man.
   - ◯ "Give your dog water food and lots of love," said the man.
   - ◯ "Give your dog water, food and lots of love, said the man."

Let's write now!

Write a **conversation** that two friends have about their pets. Use **speech marks** to show spoken words and **commas** to separate items in a list.

Glossary of terms

Adjectives describe nouns and pronouns. Types of adjectives are:

- **comparing adjectives**, e.g. quieter, quietest
- **descriptive adjectives**, e.g. short, round, little, friendly
- **number adjectives**, e.g. some, many, four.

Adverbs add meaning to verbs by telling how, where or when something is done, e.g. quickly, outside, yesterday.

Apostrophes are punctuation marks that show:

- where letters are missing in words, e.g. they're (they are)
- ownership, e.g. Jo's book (the book belonging to Jo).

Articles are the words **a**, **an** and **the**.

Commands are sentences that tell someone to do something. They usually end with a full stop (.) or sometimes an exclamation mark (!).

Commas (,) are punctuation marks that separate items in a list.

Conjunctions are words that connect single words and groups of words in sentences, e.g. and, but, or.

Contractions are words formed when two words are joined to make one, shorter word, e.g. can't (cannot). An apostrophe is used to show where the missing letters were.

Exclamations are sentences that express strong feelings. They end with an exclamation mark (!).

Nouns are naming words. They can be **singular** or **plural**, e.g. book → books. There are several types of nouns.

- **Abstract nouns** name ideas and feelings, e.g. darkness, happiness.
- **Collective nouns** name groups of people, animals, places or things, e.g. herd, flock.
- **Common nouns** name general people, animals, places or things, e.g. girl, dog, country, car.
- **Compound nouns** are formed by joining two or more words together, e.g. sunlight.
- **Proper nouns** name specific people, animals, places or things, e.g. Tom, Rover, Australia, Halloween.

Phrases are groups of words that don't make sense on their own. Usually they don't contain a verb, e.g. in the city.

Prepositions are words that connect nouns, pronouns and phrases with other words in a sentence by telling where and when, e.g. in, on, from, since, until.

Pronouns are words that are used in place of nouns. There are:

- **personal pronouns**, e.g. he, she
- **possessive pronouns**, e.g. his, her.

Questions are sentences that ask for information or opinions. They always end with a question mark (?).

Sentences are groups of words that make sense on their own. They always start with a capital letter and can end with a full stop, question mark or exclamation mark.

Speech marks are punctuation marks that are placed around spoken language, e.g. " " or ' '.

Statements are sentences that give information or opinions. They always start with a capital letter and end with a full stop.

Subjects are the people, animals or things in a sentence that do the action.

Tense shows when an action takes place, in the **present**, **past** or **future**, e.g. walk, walked, will walk.

Verbs are words that show what people, animals or things do. Types of verbs are:

- **being and having verbs**, e.g. is, was, has, had
- **doing verbs**, e.g. run
- **helping verbs**, e.g. can, will
- **saying and thinking verbs**, e.g. whispered, thought.

Answers

Unit 1 Back to school

Let's find them! (page 1)

1 Luiz was waiting for me at the gate.
2 We took our bags to the Year 3 classrooms.
3 I sat next to Luiz.

Let's go to the next step! (page 2)

1 Our teacher has already taken the roll.
2 The students returned to their classrooms.
3 The poster about sentences fell off the wall.
4 The science projects are on display in the library.
5 The Year 3 boys are practising their soccer skills.
6 Most of the teachers park their cars in the car park.
7 The circus performers are visiting the school.

Let's aim high now! (page 2)

1 Amanda and Lara are the cleverest girls in the class.
2 Mrs Harvey is the principal of our school.
3 My parents are speaking to my teacher about my work.
4 Some people from the Department of Health told us about the importance of hygiene.
5 The sports teacher explained the rules of basketball to us.
6 The new library books are on the shelves.
7 The music room is next to the hall.

Let's find them! (page 3)

1 Mum **2** The secretary **3** The girls **4** My teacher **5** hugged **6** noticed **7** played

Let's go to the next step! (page 4)

1 practise **2** eat **3** pack **4** wears **5** sits **6** write **7** share

Let's aim high now! (page 4)

1 Max asks the teacher for a pencil.
2 She drinks water from the bubbler.
3 The girls take the note to the office.
4 Mahli reads a new book every week.
5 We play handball on the playground.
6 I put my school bag next to my desk.
7 My friends help me with my homework.

Let's put it together now! (page 5)

My speech was about snakes**. I** took my pet python to school in a bag**. My** teacher pulled my name out of the box and I went to the front of the class**. I** put the bag on my teacher's desk**. My** python started to move around**. He** poked his head out of the bag**. My** teacher fainted**.**

Let's have fun! (page 5)

1 **A/The boy** threw the ball through the classroom window.
A/The girl spilled water all over her desk.
A/The spider was sitting on the classroom wall.
A/The bird hopped into our classroom.
2 The teacher **writes/is writing on the board**.
The girl **reads/is reading a book**.
The boy **waits/is waiting for the bus**.
The students **put up/raise/are putting up/are raising their hands**.

Let's have a test! (page 6)

1 Our teacher marks our books.
2 painted
3 that
4 The Year 3s and 4s
5 The new girl
6 Lots people
7 read
8 fell

Unit 2 Friends and family

Let's find them! (page 7)

The statements are all the sentences that end with full stops (.).
The questions are all the sentences that end with question marks (?).

Let's go to the next step! (page 8)

1 Most **2** Which **3** Will **4** Grandpa **5** My **6** How **7** What

Let's aim high now! (page 8)

1 How many people are there in your family?
2 Who is the best ice skater in Dad's family?
3 Is Arista the best friend you've ever had?
4 Where did you meet your best friend, Jono?
5 Does Nikita have lots of friends at school?
6 What is your brother doing?
7 Why is Mum going to the supermarket?

Let's find them! (page 9)

The exclamations are:

1 What a cool bike!
2 I can't wait to show it to my other friends!
3 How amazing is it that we have our birthdays in the same month!

The commands are:

4 Turn right and keep walking until you come to the big rock.
5 Look under the little ledge at the bottom of the rock.
6 Wait until you're sitting in your favourite chair before you open it.
7 Tell me what you think of your present.

Let's go to the next step! (page 10)

1 Help **2** Take **3** Phone **4** Tidy **5** What **6** We **7** How

Let's aim high now! (page 10)

1 Take out the garbage. – What a disgusting job!
2 Read this book to your little sister. – What a silly story!
3 Taste this chocolate cake. – How delicious is that!
4 Get ready for the party. – I'm so excited!
5 Switch off the TV. – This is such a good program!
6 Eat your broccoli. – I hate vegetables!
7 Try spelling the word again. – I'll never get it right!

Let's put it together now! (page 11)

When are you coming to stay with us again**?** We had such fun the last time you were here**.** Do you remember the time we fell in the mud**?** That was so funny**!** Mum says that next time you come to stay with us we might go camping**.** Have you ever been camping before**?** Write and let me know**.**

Let's have fun! (page 11)

1 You could share your choc-chip cookie with me.
2 Girl on left: I'm so cross!
Boy looking in packet: What a surprise!
Girl on right: How disgusting!
Boy to one side: It's so funny!
3 Picture 1: Set the table.
Picture 2: Wash the dishes.
Picture 3: Wipe the counters.

Let's have a test! (page 12)

1 I'm only eight years old and I already have a niece and a nephew.
2 Is my aunt's son my cousin?
3 ?
4 Give the newspaper to Dad.
5 My friends are awesome!
6 **.** (full stop)
7 "Is Gran coming to stay with us?"
8 "I love my dad's new car!"

Unit 3 Holiday fun!

Let's find them! (page 13)

1 mum/dad/sister **2** giraffe **3** seal **4** enclosure **5** restaurant **6** ice-cream **7** car

Let's go to the next step! (page 14)

1 shark **2** suitcase **3** hotel **4** waiter **5** ticket **6** island **7** eagle

Let's aim high now! (page 14)

People: sailor, chef, pilot , tourist, diver, mother, lifeguard
Animals: koala, kookaburra, snake, wombat, dingo, monkey, fish
Places: park, beach, country, shop, city, forest, museum
Things: umbrella, computer, seat, train, rock, book, window

Let's find them! (page 15)

1 April **2** Golden Surf **3** Thunder River Rapids Ride *or* Reef Diver **4** Castaway Bay **5** Sesame Street **6** Elmo **7** Disneyland

Let's go to the next step! (page 16)

1 Tuesday **2** Tom **3** Botanic Gardens **4** Canberra **5** Murray River **6** July **7** Banksia Street

Let's aim high now! (page 16)

1 I saw a lot of interesting fish there. – Waterside Aquarium
2 It is the smallest state in Australia. – Tasmania
3 My best friend came on holiday with us. – Lucy

4 We dressed up and went trick-or-treating. – Halloween
5 Last year we visited Australia's biggest city. – Sydney
6 It was the best time of the year to see the wildflowers. – October
7 In the holidays I watched a movie about my favourite fairytale character. – Snow White

Let's put it together now! (page 17)

Friday, Alicia Street, park, school, Juju, ball, Lilypad Pond

Let's have fun! (page 17)

Across: 1 possum 3 Victoria 4 salad 5 Cairns 6 Darwin 7 Daintree
Down: 1 passenger 2 station

Let's have a test! (page 18)

1 guest, visitor, traveller, sightseer 2 continent 3 cabin 4 passport 5 Mars 6 Eiffel Tower 7 Great Ocean road 8 Memorial, Canberra, place

Unit 4 In the wild

Let's find them! (page 19)

1 a herd of zebras 2 a swarm of gnats 3 a flock of birds 4 a troop of monkeys 5 sunlight 6 butterfly 7 grasshopper

Let's go to the next step! (page 20)

1 In California we came across a den of rattlesnakes.
2 We collected a bundle of firewood and stacked it next to our tent.
3 A patch of wildflowers was the only bit of colour in the brown field.
4 At the beach we saw a flock of seagulls circling around a fishing boat.
5 When we looked over the side of the boat, we saw a school of jellyfish.
6 When we saw Jin Ho's album of photographs, we all wanted to go to Africa.
7 The prickle of hedgehogs crossing the road looked like moving pincushions!

Let's aim high now! (page 20)

1 sunglasses (compound noun)
2 library (collective noun)
3 pod (collective noun)
4 rainforest (compound noun)
5 riverbed (compound noun)
6 pack (collective noun)
7 herd (collective noun)

Let's find them! (page 21)

1 excitement 2 curiosity 3 thrill 4 amazement 5 smell 6 joy 7 disappointment

Let's go to the next step! (page 22)

1 sorrow 2 love 3 interest 4 courage 5 relief 6 sympathy 7 tension

Let's aim high now! (page 22)

1 over the moon (happiness)
2 think the world of my mum (admiration)
3 makes my hair stand on end (fear)
4 makes my flesh crawl (disgust)
5 butterflies in my tummy (nervousness)
6 down in the dumps (sadness)
7 makes my blood boil (anger)

Let's put it together now! (page 23)

Paul and Marcie were picking a bunch of flowers for Mum. Suddenly they heard a buzzing sound. They looked up and got a huge fright when they saw a swarm of bees heading towards them. Paul grabbed Marcie and pulled her towards the pathway. They ran as fast as they could, but they could still hear the bees behind them. Then a flock of birds came out of nowhere. To the children's surprise, the buzzing stopped. Paul and Marcie walked back to the playground where Mum and Alex were waiting for them.

Let's have fun! (page 23)

1 a squirm of earthworms, a squawk of cockatoos, a tickle of feathers
2 treehouse, seahorse, starfish
3 Picture 1: fear, Picture 2: uncertainty, Picture 3: pleasure

Let's have a test! (page 24)

1 army
2 The white rhino is in danger of becoming extinct.
3 seaside
4 I wouldn't like to run out of water in the desert.
5 delight
6 The conservationist looked worried.
7 swordfish
8 calmness

Unit 5 Hobbies and interests

Let's find them! (page 25)
1 cars 2 boxes 3 superheroes 4 figures 5 games 6 walruses 7 witches

Let's go to the next step! (page 26)
1 books 2 cards 3 crayons 4 buses 5 leashes 6 branches 7 bushes 8 churches 9 buzzes 10 crosses 11 dresses 12 volcanoes 13 cargoes 14 tomatoes

Let's aim high now! (page 26)
1 matches 2 hairbrushes 3 tricks 4 animals 5 potatoes 6 dominoes 7 dishes

Let's find them! (page 27)
1 ladies 2 fairies 3 elves 4 men 5 teeth 6 people 7 sheep

Let's go to the next step! (page 28)
1 jellies 2 supplies 3 berries 4 curries 5 babies 6 cities 7 lollies 8 flies 9 calves 10 leaves 11 shelves 12 mice 13 women 14 furniture

Let's aim high now! (page 28)
2 ponies 3 loaves 4 geese 5 daisies 6 babies 7 goldfish 8 sand

Let's put it together now! (page 29)
hobbies, socks, loaves, hutches, jewellery, potatoes, people

Let's have fun! (page 29)

x	z	g	l	a	s	s	e	s	v	s	w
a	p	u	j	q	f	e	j	x	v	e	k
d	a	f	s	g	u	r	j	s	r	h	c
k	i	s	x	a	m	p	s	y	j	c	n
m	n	p	q	z	t	e	a	o	j	t	l
c	t	o	t	g	s	h	m	t	d	a	j
a	i	s	n	o	w	g	l	o	b	e	s
r	n	f	b	z	z	b	c	x	x	q	r
d	g	a	l	s	c	i	m	o	c	l	u
s	s	w	d	g	j	b	s	h	s	m	s
d	h	y	k	l	f	i	d	v	q	a	n
s	d	i	d	g	e	r	i	d	o	o	s

Let's have a test! (page 30)
1 My little sister loves to play with blocks.
2 I have a collection of wooden foxes.
3 My dad's hobby is growing potatoes.
4 My mum makes us fancy lollies.
5 I cut the lump of clay into two halves.
6 Some people collect rabbits' feet.
7 scissors
8 pants

Unit 6 Tasty treats!

Let's find them! (page 31)
1 it 2 I 3 She 4 He 5 We 6 they 7 yourself

Let's go to the next step! (page 32)
1 me 2 you 3 him 4 ourselves 5 us 6 them 7 themselves

Let's aim high now! (page 32)
1 She 2 them 3 He 4 You 5 it 6 we 7 her

Let's find them! (page 33)
Choose seven of these: mine, hers, his, theirs, ours, your, their, my, yours

Let's go to the next step! (page 34)
1 mine 2 its 3 their 4 his 5 Our/Their/His/Her 6 ours 7 her

Let's aim high now! (page 34)
1 mine 2 its 3 hers 4 yours 5 their 6 theirs 7 her

Let's put it together now! (page 35)
your gobstoppers, his mouth, her exploding gobstoppers, We have the tastiest, think they have, Ours are better, for yourself

Let's have fun! (page 35)
1 I ate the pizza slice because it was mine.
2 The cereal is in its usual place in the cupboard.
3 She would not finish her broccoli.
4 Mum was cross with him because he ate all the spaghetti.
5 My chocolate cake is sweeter than hers.

Let's have a test! (page 36)
1 I will buy them an ice-cream when we go to the shops.
2 Me likes sweet food and him likes savoury food.
3 himself

4 us
5 My dad makes his own sausages.
6 Your blueberry muffins have more fruit in them than their.
7 ours
8 Her, his

Unit 7 Interesting characters

Let's find them! (page 37)
1 white 2 wrinkled 3 small 4 pointed 5 blue 6 terrible 7 sad

Let's go to the next step! (page 38)
1 huge 2 pink 3 puffy 4 loud 5 crooked 6 kind 7 unhappy

Let's aim high now! (page 38)
1 evil – wicked 2 brilliant – excellent 3 horrible – awful 4 brave – courageous 5 mischievous – naughty 6 handsome – good-looking 7 dangerous – risky

Let's find them! (page 39)
1 older 2 weirdest 3 scarier 4 taller, shorter 5 smallest, largest

Let's go to the next step! (page 40)

One character	Two characters	More than two characters
quiet	quieter	quietest
strong	stronger	strongest
large	larger	largest
happy	happier	happiest
thin	thinner	thinnest
mean	meaner	meanest
wild	wilder	wildest
cruel	crueller	cruellest

Let's aim high now! (page 40)
1 cleverest 2 prettier 3 tiniest 4 uglier 5 grander 6 hungriest 7 biggest

Let's put it together now! (page 41)
biggest, big, hairy, small, smaller, louder, heaviest

Let's have fun! (page 41)
friendly, jealous, scared, excited, nasty, sad, happy, fancy, calm

Let's have a test! (page 42)
1 Toto is Dorothy's adorable dog in *The Wizard of Oz*.
2 I have just read a book about witches and wizards.
3 yellow
4 square
5 The wizard's house was bigger than the witch's.
6 The naughty girl in this story is always in trouble.
7 smallest, darkest
8 wiser

Unit 8 Caring for the environment

Let's find them! (page 43)
1 more 2 One/second 3 fifty 4 third 5 no 6 A 7 the

Let's go to the next step! (page 44)
1 all 2 The 3 The 4 some 5 seven 6 first 7 Most

Let's aim high now! (page 44)
1 few 2 One 3 Some/The 4 an 5 three 6 any 7 the/some

Let's find them! (page 45)
2 the younger children
3 a few bushes
4 the grey concrete wall
5 some pretty, colourful flowers
6 a better environment
7 some interesting wildlife

Let's go to the next step! (page 46)
1 two little bushes
2 the ugly weeds
3 my little vegetable patch
4 the old newspapers
5 a small concrete birdbath
6 ten green, shady trees
7 my favourite park

Let's aim high now! (page 46)
1 We collect rainwater in a big green tank.
2 They saved the two little joeys whose mother died.
3 Birds like to live in large, leafy trees.
4 I will recycle the glass bottles.
5 We told them not to use all the water.
6 The smoke comes from five old factories.
7 A few kind people helped us clear away the rubbish.

Let's put it together now! (page 47)

a very precious resource, All living things, An important thing, the/any/all leaking taps, these two things, many/some other things, a shorter time

Let's have fun! (page 47)

so much garbage; too many long, hot showers; the city streets; a compost bin; a leaking tap; the washing machine; both sides of the page; all wet clothes

Let's have a test! (page 48)

1 an 2 the 3 fifth 4 any 5 one
6 a new bicycle
7 energy-saving light bulbs
8 I use the large green grocery bags when I go shopping.

Unit 9 Doing the right thing

Let's find them! (page 49)

1 eat 2 disturb 3 Greet 4 Keep 5 Raise 6 speak 7 treat

Let's go to the next step! (page 50)

1 help 2 Put 3 stand 4 Eat 5 Wait 6 Clean, make 7 Answer, asks

Let's aim high now! (page 50)

1 try 2 play 3 sweep 4 tidy 5 shares 6 thank 7 push

Let's find them! (page 51)

1 is 2 could 3 should 4 must 5 are 6 has 7 will

Let's go to the next step! (page 52)

1 will 2 must 3 has 4 could 5 may 6 were 7 should

Let's aim high now! (page 52)

2 was trying 3 are working 4 will let 5 did take 6 do like 7 have seen

Let's put it together now! (page 53)

Do not kick balls near windows.
Do not fight with your friends.
Bad behaviour is not allowed.
Share your toys with your friends.
Ask before taking food from the fridge.
You must clean up if you make a mess.
Thank your friends for coming to play with you.

Let's have fun! (page 53)

s	x	g	h	z	m	u	s	t	p
h	s	t	j	u	q	j	m	y	u
o	r	z	s	a	d	m	v	l	e
u	m	b	h	a	v	e	t	y	n
l	i	r	p	w	i	n	t	p	e
d	g	d	e	n	e	r	o	g	t
r	h	c	s	q	v	d	z	t	s
c	t	o	d	h	y	r	t	k	i
x	r	u	w	p	d	a	v	j	l
c	a	r	e	e	p	l	e	h	r

Let's have a test! (page 54)

1 greets 2 lend 3 Step 4 Walk 5 does 6 has
7 They should care for their pets.
8 She helps me with the task.

Unit 10 Sporting heroes

Let's find them! (page 55)

1 cheered 2 say 3 announced 4 whispered 5 exclaimed 6 told 7 replied

Let's go to the next step! (page 56)

1 moaned 2 promised 3 explained 4 grumbled 5 murmured 6 coughed 7 warned

Let's aim high now! (page 56)

1 sighed 2 called 3 asked 4 whined 5 answered 6 argued 7 spoke

Let's find them! (page 57)

1 is 2 was 3 had 4 were 5 has 6 am 7 are 8 have

Let's go to the next step! (page 58)

1 have 2 is 3 am 4 be 5 are 6 had 7 was

Let's aim high now! (page 58)

1 are 2 been 3 was 4 were 5 is 6 has 7 be

Let's put it together now! (page 59)

Cadel Evans is one of Australia's greatest cyclists. He has admirers all over the world. This is what some people said after he won the Tour de France in 2011.
"What a fantastic cyclist!" exclaimed Mai Chan.
"Has Australia ever had a greater cyclist?" asked Josh Smith.
"I don't think there will ever be a greater cyclist," commented Robyn Dickson.

Let's have fun! (page 59)

Across: 1 stuttered 4 am 5 scold 6 had 8 sobbed
Down: 2 teased 3 demanded 7 is

Let's have a test! (page 60)

1 Many young sailors ask Jessica Watson for advice.
2 Our team tried hard but lost the match.
3 cheered
4 This is the best team in the league.
5 We watched them playing tennis.
6 were
7 He has basketball practice this afternoon.
8 had

Unit 11 The city

Let's find them! (page 61)

1 reach 2 hurry 3 flutters 4 hoot 5 whine 6 strikes 7 rumbles

Let's go to the next step! (page 62)

1 are 2 stops 3 shine 4 are dashing 5 wait 6 buy 7 were looking

Let's aim high now! (page 62)

1 show 2 have 3 eat 4 takes 5 catches 6 are 7 look

Let's find them! (page 63)

1 we'll 2 I'm 3 there'll 4 don't 5 won't 6 we'd 7 city's

Let's go to the next step! (page 64)

1 You're – You are
2 We've – We have
3 She'd – She would
4 I'd – I would
5 They've – They have
6 He's – He is
7 Doesn't – Does not

Let's aim high now! (page 64)

1 can't – cannot
2 Where's – Where is
3 they'd – they would
4 They're – They are
5 she'll – she will
6 He's – He has
7 didn't – did not

Let's put it together now! (page 65)

don't, is, I'm, make, push, they're, That's

Let's have fun! (page 65)

1 Oscar catches, Martin and Jerry clap, Veronica dances, Sarah and Alison sing
2 I haven't been to the city for a long time.
There's a shop in the city I'd like to visit.
It's not as peaceful in the city as it is in the country.
We're going to watch the procession in the city centre.

Let's have a test! (page 66)

1 She is holding an umbrella.
2 We visits the museum.
3 is, was
4 carries
5 My friend said she'd tell me where the shop was.
6 I wish the'yd told me which bus to catch.
7 I had
8 can't

Unit 12 Ways of travelling

Let's find them! (page 67)

1 bought 2 was 3 laughed 4 said 5 disagreed 6 informed 7 wasted

Let's go to the next step! (page 68)

1 went 2 glided 3 sped 4 pushed 5 was 6 caught 7 walked

Let's aim high now! (page 68)

1 were 2 went 3 sailed 4 flew 5 stopped 6 drove 7 mounted, rode

Let's find them! (page 69)

1 will build 2 will see 3 will be 4 will travel 5 will use 6 will switch 7 is going to happen

Let's go to the next step! (page 70)

1 will drive 2 will land 3 are going to hire 4 will fly 5 are going to sail 6 are going to ride 7 will transport

Let's aim high now! (page 70)

1 Next year my dad will travel/is going to travel overseas.
2 Tomorrow morning we will try out/are going to try out our new skateboards.
3 Next month my father will ride/is going to ride his bicycle to work.
4 My next racing bike will be/is going to be red, white and blue.

5 Tomorrow my brother will drive/is going to drive Nanna to the shops.
6 Next month my grandparents will stay/are going to stay in their caravan.
7 Tonight the aeroplane will take off/is going to take off with a loud roar.

Let's put it together now! (page 71)
bought, got, brought, saw, will put/is going to put, will do/am going to do, will take/is going to take

Let's have fun! (page 71)
Past tense verbs: rowed, cycled, carried, flew
Future tense verbs: are going to drive, is going to walk, will sail, will paddle

Let's have a test! (page 72)
1 Yesterday I travelled to school by bus.
2 I walked to the shops tomorrow.
3 fell
4 drift
5 The aeroplane will land early tomorrow morning.
6 Next month the train sped along the tracks.
7 are going
8 looked

Unit 13 The Dreamtime

Let's find them! (page 73)
1 kindly 2 Later 3 immediately 4 firmly 5 quickly 6 away 7 Afterwards

Let's go to the next step! (page 74)
1 here – where 2 proudly – how 3 respectfully – how 4 slowly – how 5 yesterday – when 6 always – when 7 somewhere – where

Let's aim high now! (page 74)
1 softly 2 nervously 3 again 4 inside 5 everywhere 6 never 7 still

Let's find them! (page 75)
1 in the forest
2 with a loud roar
3 around his friend
4 under the ground
5 after sunset
6 inside the sand
7 to this day

Let's go to the next step! (page 76)
1 across 2 behind 3 beside 4 before 5 to 6 with 7 into

Let's aim high now! (page 76)
1 with 2 about 3 across 4 on/across 5 since 6 in 7 down/into

Let's put it together now! (page 77)
Two men went fishing on a lake. At the end of the day, their boat was full of fish. When they got to shore, they saw a stranger walking towards them. The stranger looked hungrily at the fish, but the men refused to share them with him. The man looked at them sadly and said they were greedy. When they cleaned the fish later that day, they saw that they were full of bones.

Let's have fun! (page 77)
1 Joey fits snugly in Mother Kangaroo's pouch.
To get away from the hunters, Emu ran quickly across the open plains.
Mayra yelled furiously as he blew up a windstorm around Bilba.
The men eyed the fish greedily.
2 The hunter is throwing his spear at the kangaroo.
The platypus is swimming under the water.
The hunter is sitting beside the creek.
The wombat is waddling towards/across the creek.
The hunter is dropping his fishing line into the water.
The kookaburra is sitting on the branch.
The hunter is walking across/towards the creek.

Let's have a test! (page 78)
1 The hunter is sharpening his spear now.
2 The bilby will sleep underground.
3 The storyteller is speaking clearly.
4 easily
5 in
6 to
7 until
8 between

Unit 14 Paper magic

Let's find them! (page 79)

1 or **2** and **3** before **4** unless **5** but **6** if **7** because

Let's go to the next step! (page 80)

1 if **2** or **3** although **4** while **5** but **6** so **7** because

Let's aim high now! (page 80)

1 and **2** because **3** unless **4** so **5** when **6** but **7** or

Let's find them! (page 81)

1 the writer **2** the merchant **3** the craftsman **4** the tree **5** the bookbinders **6** the warehouses **7** the libraries

Let's go to the next step! (page 82)

1. Joseph's paper model won first prize.
2. The students' books are in their bags.
3. Melissa's paper lantern is under the desk.
4. The girl's lampshade is made of cardboard.
5. These boys' paper aeroplanes are in the bin.
6. I flipped through the book's pages to see the pictures.
7. Those artists' drawings are done on a special kind of paper.

Let's aim high now! (page 82)

1. It is Daniel's paper hat.
2. They are the boxes' labels.
3. They are the books' covers.
4. It is the printer's machine.
5. They are my grandmother's letters.
6. It is my sister's paperweight.
7. They are the teachers' bookmarks.

Let's put it together now! (page 83)

My book's pages are old **and** tattered,
But I still love it.
The title's letters are faded and dull,
but I still know what they say.
If I turn to my favourite picture
I can still hear my grandmother's voice
telling me about the dragon's treasure
in the big, wooden chest.

Let's have fun! (page 83)

1. if, but, and
2. The doll's bed is made of cardboard.
   The boy's packet is going in the bin.
   The girl drew the leaf's outline on the paper.

Let's have a test! (page 84)

1. I have paper, but I don't have a pencil.
2. We like this paper after it's red.
3. if
4. before
5. The girls' cards are in the envelopes.
6. The students books' are on the shelves.
7. lady's
8. diaries'

Unit 15 Pets

Let's find them! (page 85)

1. "Should we get a dog or a cat?"
2. "Dogs are a lot of work."
3. "They're more fun to play with."
4. "Cats can be fun too,"
5. "and they're cuter than dogs."
6. "Oh, no!"
7. "Little dogs are much cuter than cats!"

Let's go to the next step! (page 86)

1. "Look at the cute little puppy!" exclaimed Jodie.
2. "Take your dog for regular walks," advised the vet.
3. Tina said, "I would rather have a canary than a mouse."
4. "How many fish have you bought for the fish tank?" asked Kamal.
5. Monica shouted, "Be careful you don't step on my pet chameleon!"
6. "I have two hermit crabs that I keep in a tank," Nick told his teacher.
7. "When are you taking your poodle to the dog parlour?" Natasha asked.

Let's aim high now! (page 86)

1. "That's the puppy I want!" exclaimed Kim.
2. "What is your parrot's name?" asked Ricky.
3. "You are my best friend," said Tilda to her puppy.
4. "My cat's favourite food is roast chicken," said Cara.
5. "My cat coughed up a fur ball this morning," laughed Lena.
6. "Did you know that Josh has stick insects for pets?" asked Hugo.

7 Martin announced, "I am going to the pet shop to buy my dog a new collar."

Let's find them! (page 87)

1 Spiky, Skinny and Scary
2 cheese, tuna and chicken
3 a jacket, bow tie and hat
4 a cushion, blanket or mat
5 fingers, wrists and arms
6 a gerbil, a budgie or a rat
7 Elmo, Ernie or Oscar

Let's go to the next step! (page 88)

1 I gave the kittens to Micky, Kyle and Cassie.
2 My favourite birds are budgies, parrots and cockatoos.
3 He has bought his dog a bed, a collar and some snacks.
4 I may get a puppy, a kitten or a guinea pig for my birthday.
5 My cousin lives on a farm and has a horse, a pony and a pig.
6 There is a mattress, a blanket and a pillow in my dog's kennel.
7 When we go on holiday, my cat stays with my aunt, my gran or my friend.

Let's aim high now! (page 88)

1 My dogs' names are Reggie, Max and Molly.
2 I throw a ball, stick or soft toy for my dog to fetch.
3 My favourite dogs are poodles, spaniels and labradors.
4 I buy my cat's food from a pet shop, supermarket or vet.
5 At the pet shop I saw goldfish, mice, hamsters and birds.
6 He might buy his kitten a toy, a cushion or a scratching post.
7 We've taken our pets with us to Melbourne, Brisbane, Sydney and Perth.

Let's put it together now! (page 89)

"Why can't I have a dog, Mum?" asked Amanda.
"It costs a lot of money to look after a dog," replied Mum.
"We already have a bed, bowl and kennel for a dog," said Amanda.
"That's from when Gran, Gramps and Aunt Jo were staying here with their dog," said Mum. "There are also lots of other things to buy for dogs."
"Like what?" asked Amanda.
"Like food, medicines and toys," said Mum.

Let's have fun! (page 89)

1 Christine: May I hold your puppy?
Miles: Yes, but be careful.
2 a cage, a kennel and a fish tank
a dog collar, a leash and a bowl
a boy, a girl and a kitten
a lizard, a snake and a turtle
a hen, an egg and a chick

Let's have a test! (page 90)

1 Tracey said, "What a cute puppy!"
2 The vet said, Chocolate is bad for dogs."
3 "I am going to take my dog for a walk," said Jerry.
4 Dimitri said, "I have two pets—a dog and a cat."
5 They have rabbits, gerbils, mice and chickens.
6 We took our dog, cat, canary and pet mouse with us on holiday.
7 "Give your dog water, food and lots of love," said the man.

Notes